FOR ORGANS, PIANOS & ELECTRONIC KEYBOARDS

E-Z PLAY TODAY

95

MOVIE SELECTIONS
from
THE PHANTOM OF THE OPERA

ISBN 978-1-4234-0583-2

HAL•LEONARD®
CORPORATION

7777 W. BLUEMOUND RD. P.O. BOX 13819 MILWAUKEE, WI 53213

Visit Hal Leonard Online at
www.halleonard.com

Published by
The Really Useful Group Limited
22 Tower Street, London WC2H 9TW
www.reallyuseful.com

Exclusively Distributed By

7777 W. Bluemound Rd. P.O. Box 13819 Milwaukee, WI 53213

ISBN: 1-4234-0583-8

This edition is comprised of works written for the original stage production of
THE PHANTOM OF THE OPERA
together with three new works, 'The Fairground', 'Journey To The Cemetery'
and 'Learn To Be Lonely', which were specifically written for the movie.

Photographs by Alex Bailey

Book designed by Dewynters, London

Think of Me

Registration 3
Rhythm: 8 Beat, Pops, or Rock

Music by Andrew Lloyd Webber
Lyrics by Charles Hart
Additional Lyrics by Richard Stilgoe

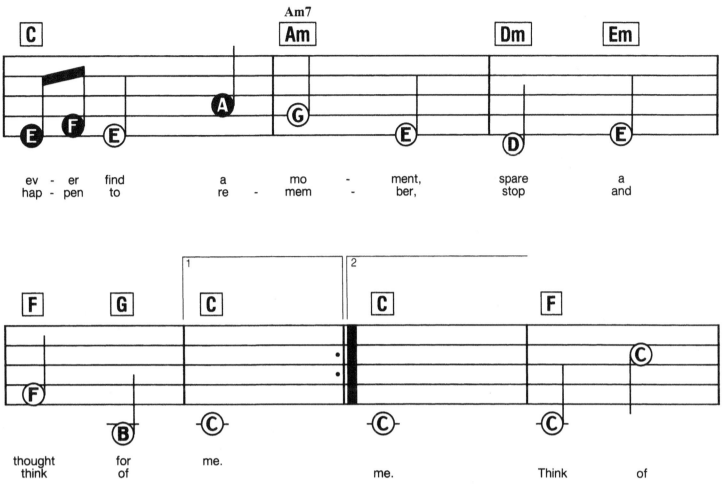

ev - er find   a   mo - ment,   spare   a
hap - pen to   re - mem - ber,   stop   and

thought for   me.
think   for of   me.   Think   of

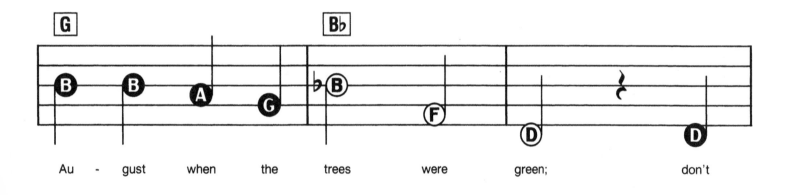

Au - gust when the trees were green;   don't

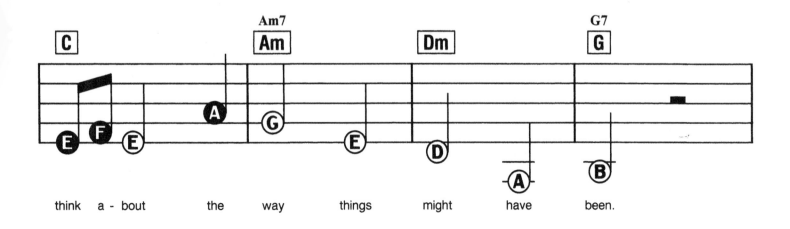

think a - bout the way things might have been.

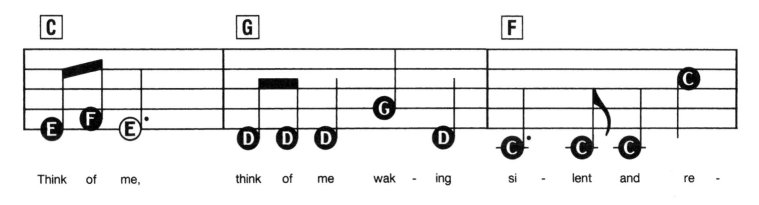

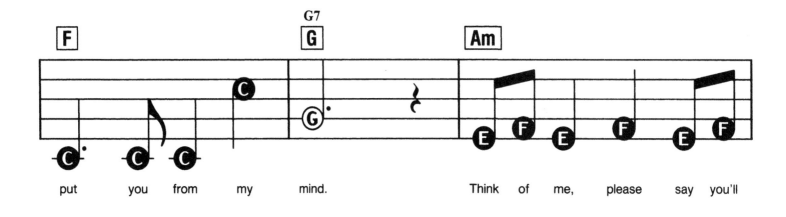

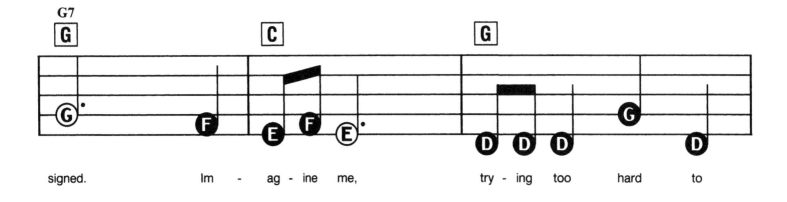

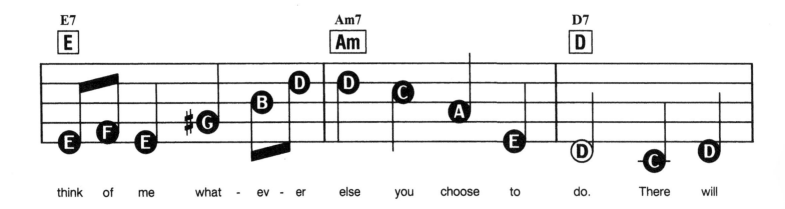

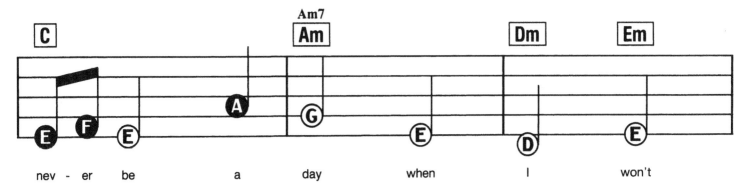

nev - er be a day when I won't

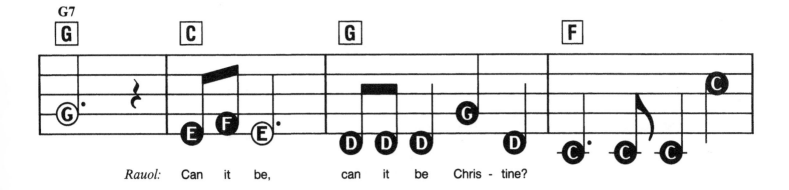

think of you. *(Instrumental)*

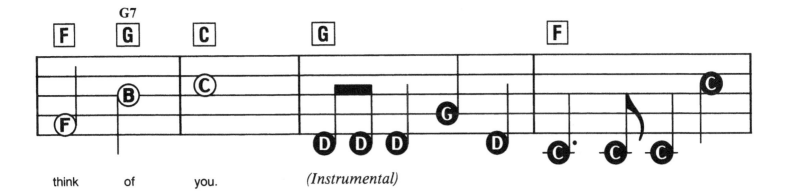

Rauol: Can it be, can it be Chris - tine?

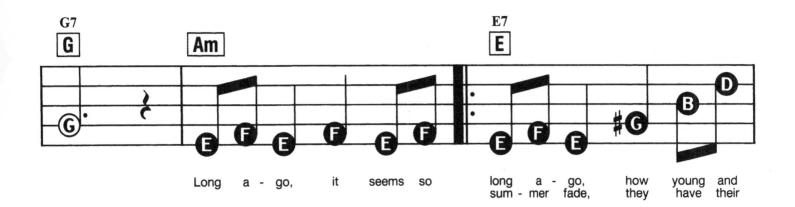

Long a - go, it seems so long a - go, how young and
sum - mer fade, they have their

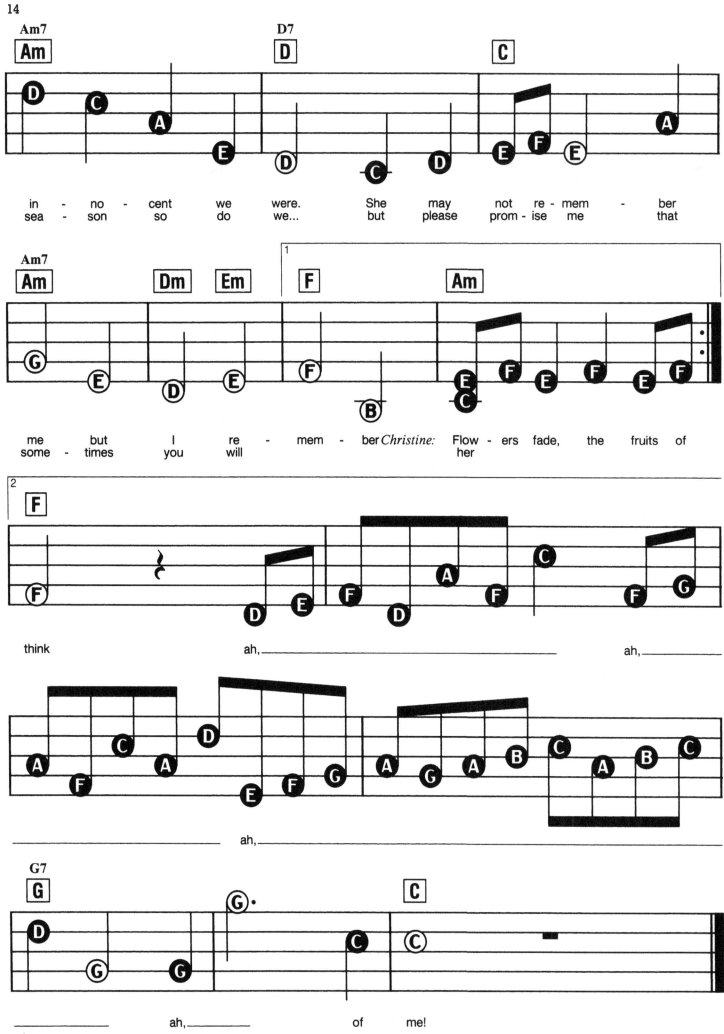

The Phantom of the Opera

Music by Andrew Lloyd Webber
Lyrics by Charles Hart
Additional Lyrics by Richard Stilgoe and Mike Batt

Registration 6
Rhythm: Disco, 8 Beat, or Rock

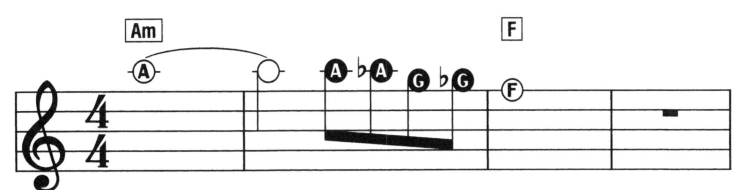

(Instrumental Solo)

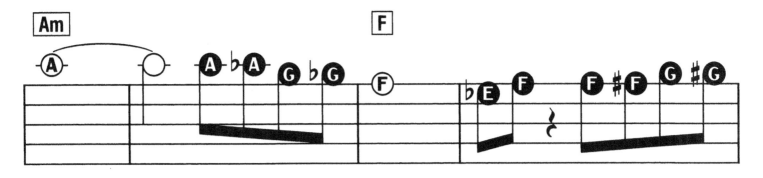

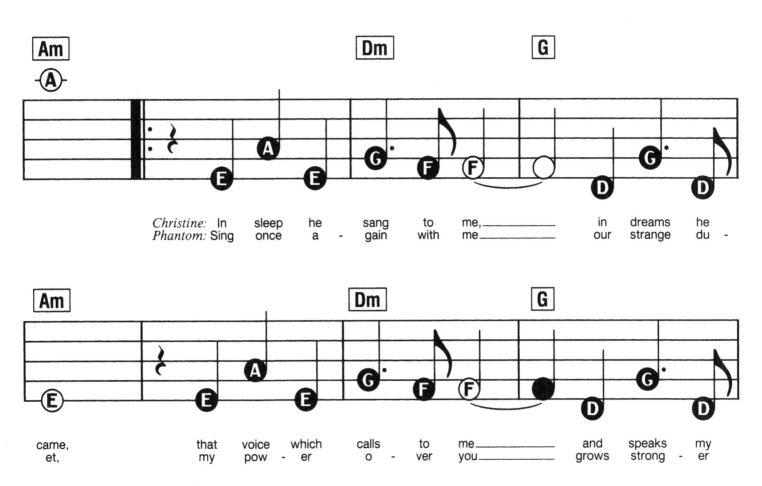

Christine: In sleep he sang to me, _____ in dreams he
Phantom: Sing once a - gain with me _____ our strange du -

came, that voice which calls to me _____ and speaks my
et, my pow - er o - ver you _____ grows strong - er

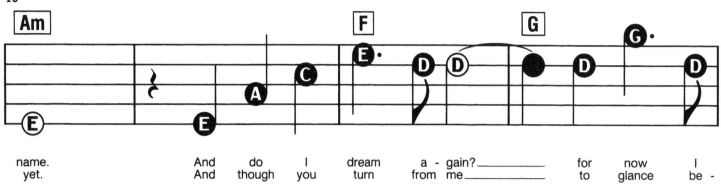

name.   And   do   I   dream   a - gain?_____   for   now   I
yet.   And though you   turn   from me_____   to   glance   be -

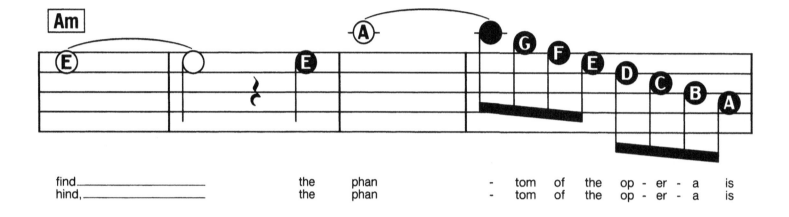

find_____   the   phan - tom of the op - er - a   is
hind,_____   the   phan - tom of the op - er - a   is

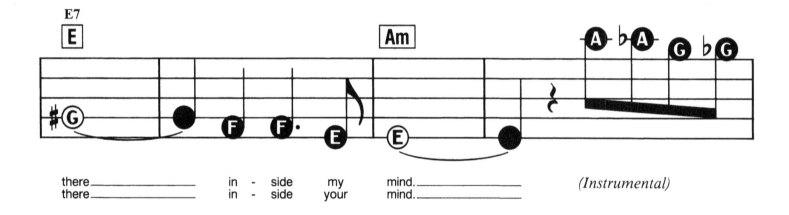

there_____   in - side my   mind._____   *(Instrumental)*
there_____   in - side your mind._____

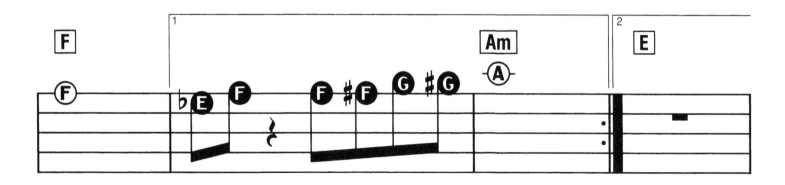

0

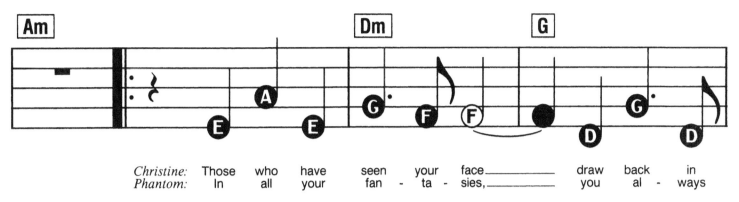

Christine: Those who have seen your face draw back in
Phantom: In all your fan - ta - sies, you al - ways

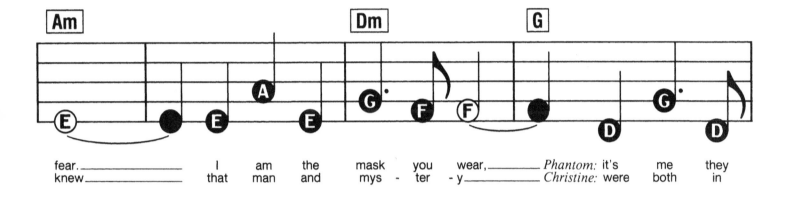

fear. I am the mask you wear, Phantom: it's me they
knew that man and mys - ter - y Christine: were both in

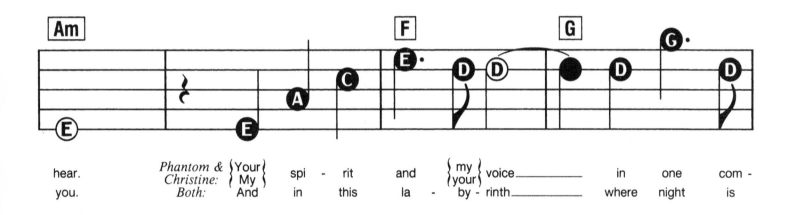

hear. Phantom & Christine: {Your/My} spi - rit and {my/your} voice in one com -
you. Both: And in this la - by - rinth where night is

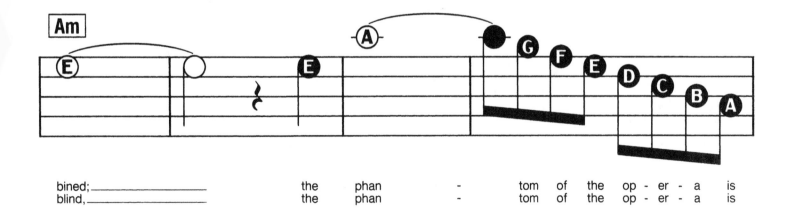

bined; the phan - tom of the op - er - a is
blind, the phan - tom of the op - er - a is

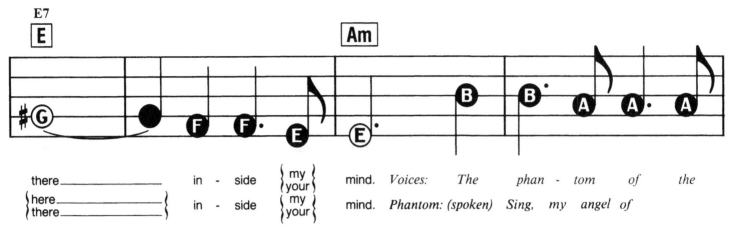

there_____ in - side { my / your } mind. *Voices: The phan - tom of the*
here_____ in - side { my / your } mind. *Phantom: (spoken) Sing, my angel of*
there_____

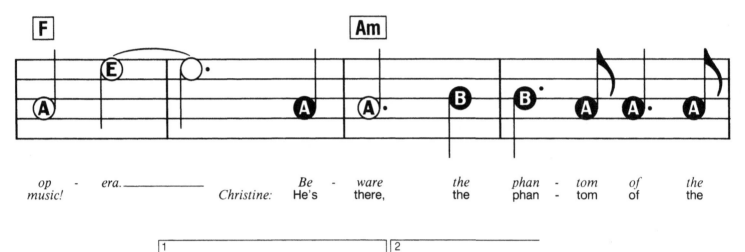

op - era._____ *Christine:* Be - ware the phan - tom of the
music! He's there, the phan - tom of the

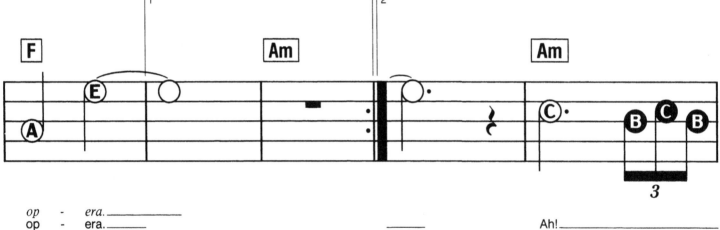

op - era._____
op - era._____ Ah!_____

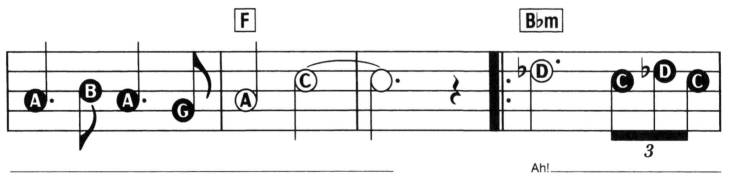

Ah!_____

Phantom: (spoken) Sing, my angel, sing!

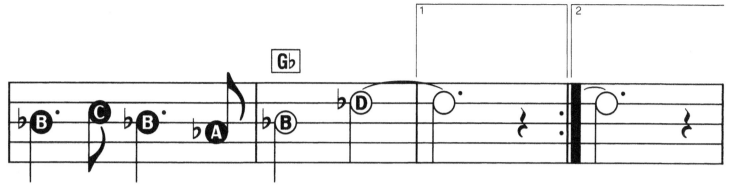

(First time:) Sing for me!

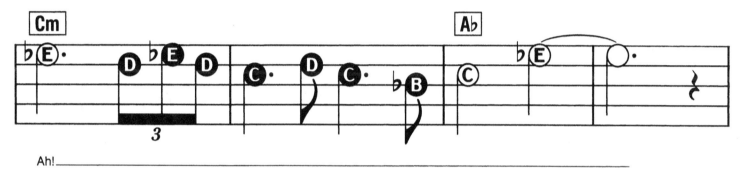

Ah!

Phantom: Sing, my angel of music!

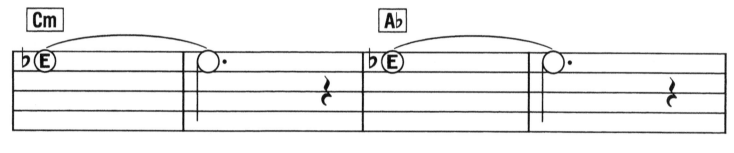

Ah!   Ah!

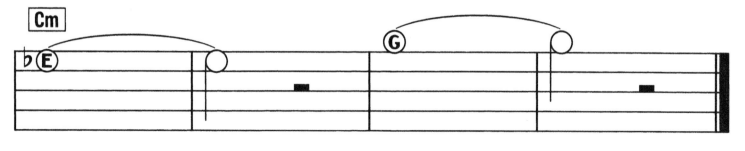

Ah!   Ah!

Angel of Music

Registration 1
Rhythm: Waltz

Music by Andrew Lloyd Webber
Lyrics by Charles Hart
Additional Lyrics by Richard Stilgoe

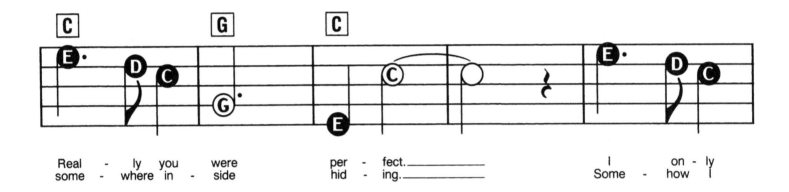

Meg: Where in the world have you been hid - ing?
Here in this world room he calls me soft - ly,

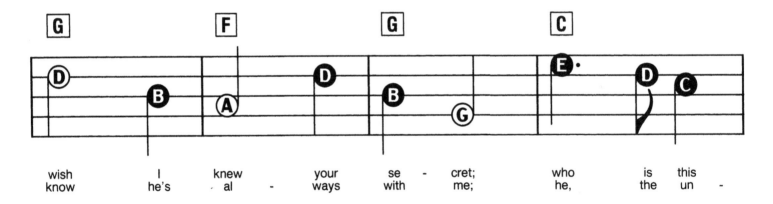

Real - ly you were per - fect. I on - ly
some - where in - side hid - ing. Some - how I

wish I knew your se - cret; who is this
know he's al - ways with me; he, the un -

new tu - tor? Christine: Fa - ther once
seen gen - ius. Meg: I watched your

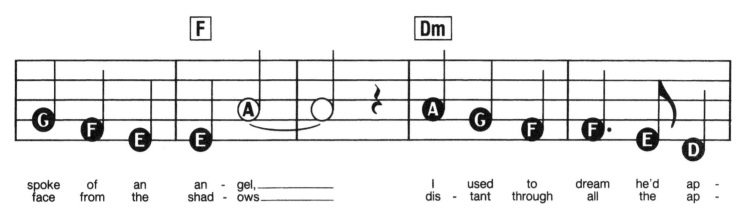

spoke   of   an   an - gel,_____   I   used   to   dream   he'd   ap -
face   from   the   shad - ows_____   dis - tant   through   all   the   ap -

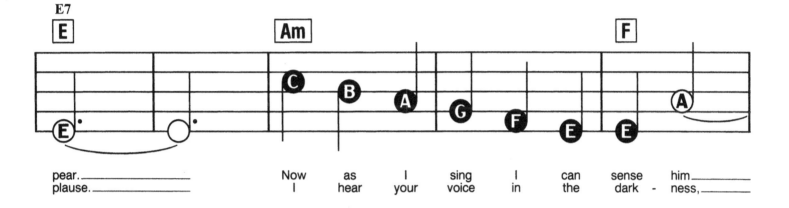

pear._____   Now   as   I   sing   I   can   sense   him_____
plause._____   I   hear   your   voice   in   the   dark - ness,_____

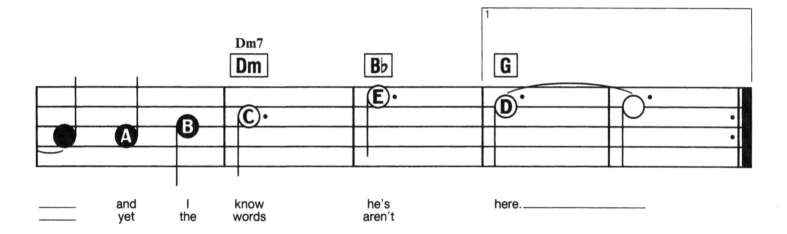

_____   and   I   know   he's   here._____
_____   yet   the   words   aren't

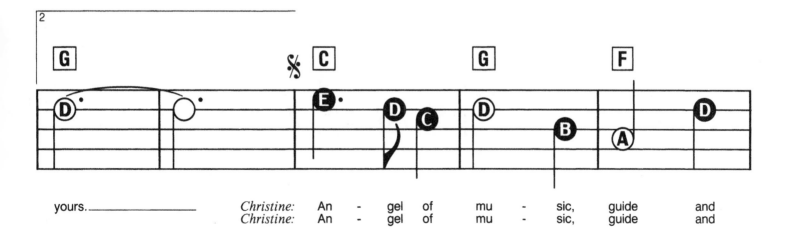

yours._____   *Christine:* An - gel   of   mu - sic,   guide   and
                     Christine: An - gel   of   mu - sic,   guide   and

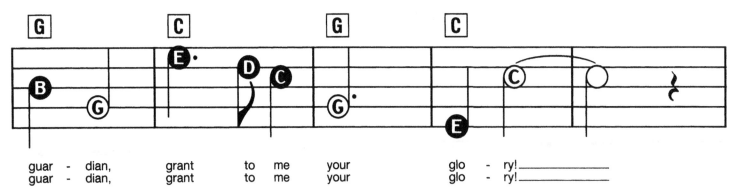

guar - dian, grant to me your glo - ry!_____
guar - dian, grant to me your glo - ry!_____

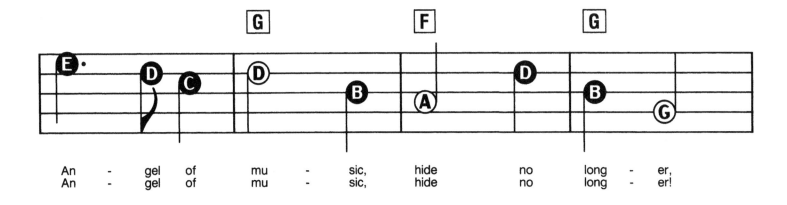

An - gel of mu - sic, hide no long - er,
An - gel of mu - sic, hide no long - er!

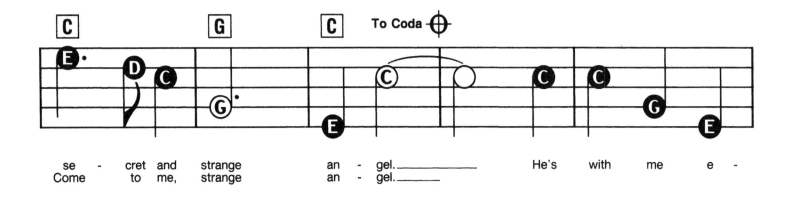

To Coda ⊕

se - cret and strange an - gel._____ He's with me e -
Come to me, strange an - gel._____

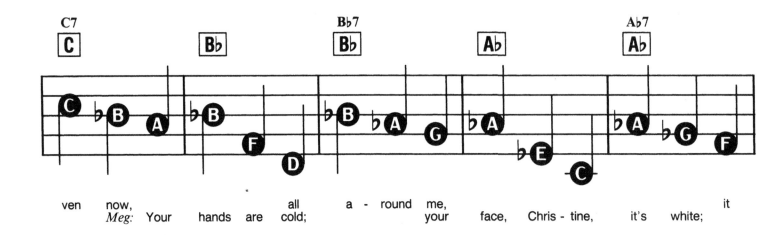

ven now, Your hands are all a - round me, it
Meg: Your hands are cold; your face, Chris - tine, it's white;

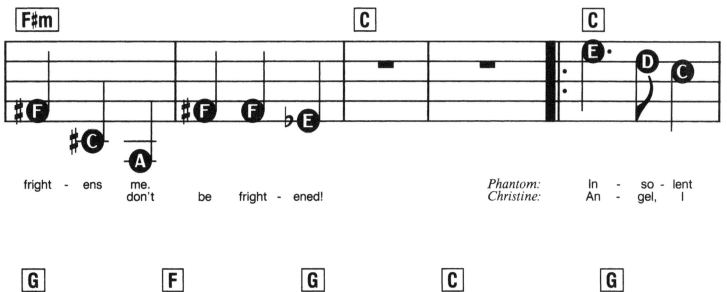

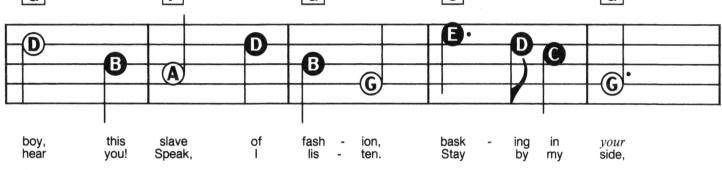

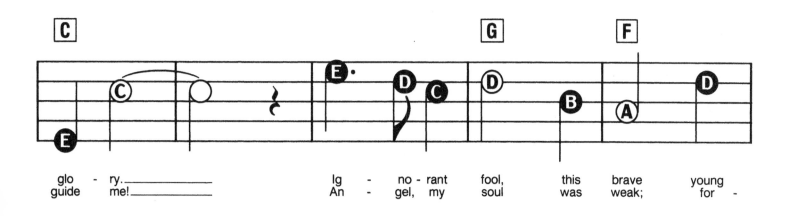

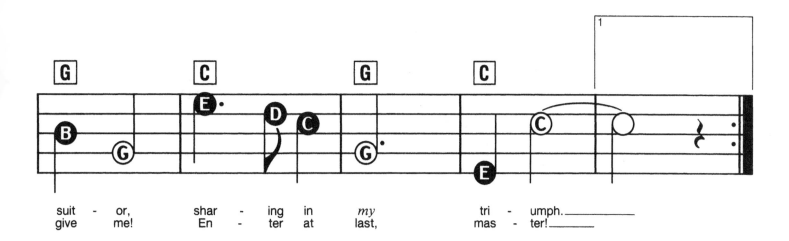

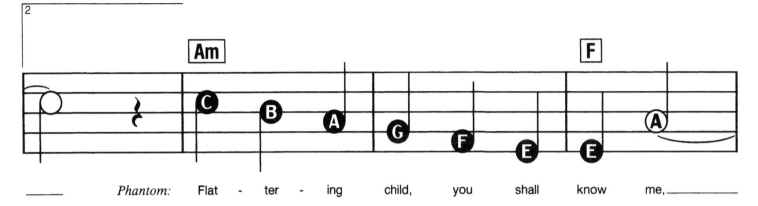

Phantom: Flat - ter - ing child, you shall know me, _____

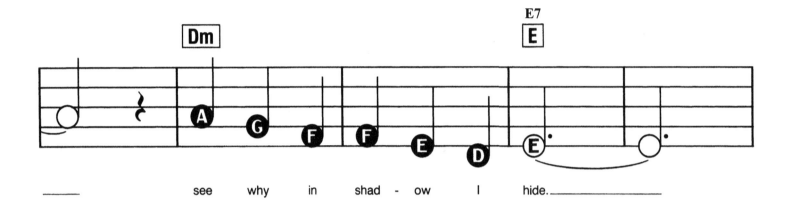

_____ see why in shad - ow I hide. _____

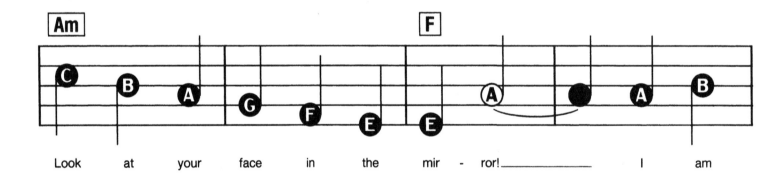

Look at your face in the mir - ror! _____ I am

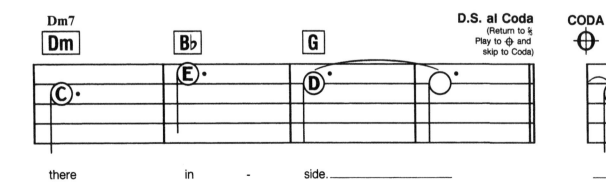

there in - side. _____ _____

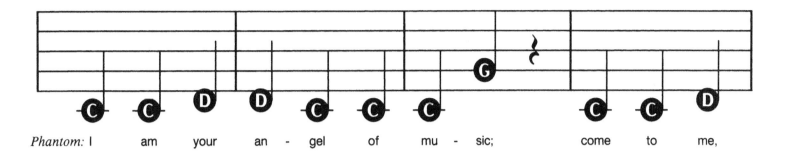

Phantom: I am your an - gel of mu - sic; come to me,

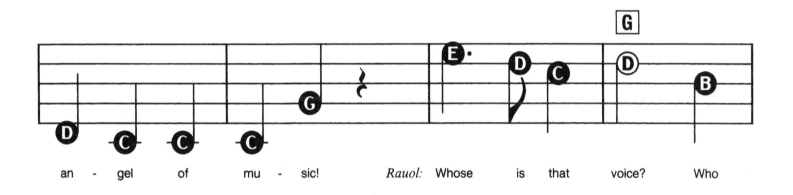

an - gel of mu - sic! *Rauol:* Whose is that voice? Who

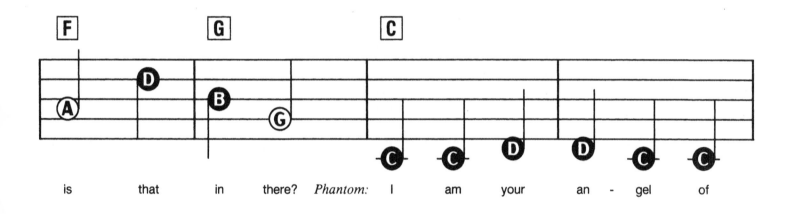

is that in there? *Phantom:* I am your an - gel of

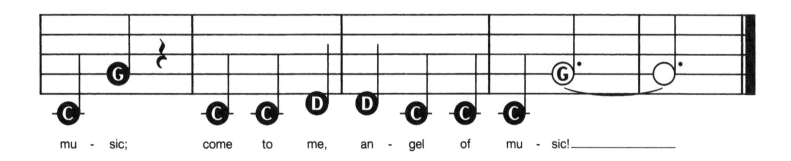

mu - sic; come to me, an - gel of mu - sic!_____

The Music of the Night

Registration 10
Rhythm: 8 Beat or Rock

Music by Andrew Lloyd Webber
Lyrics by Charles Hart
Additional Lyrics by Richard Stilgoe

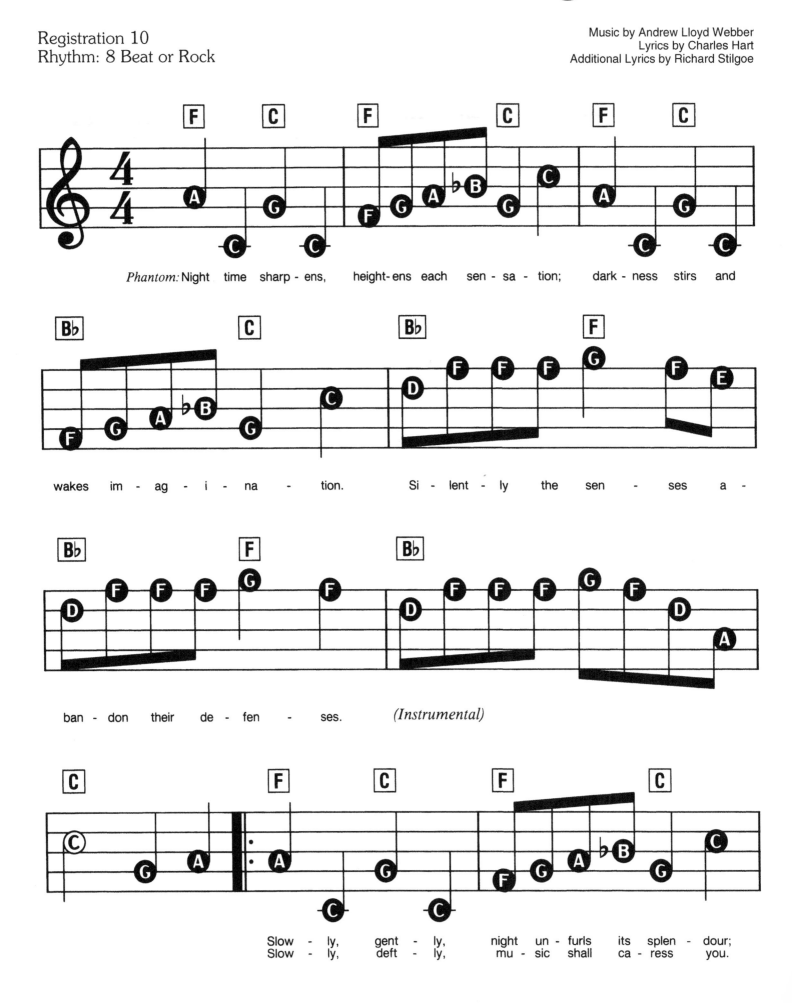

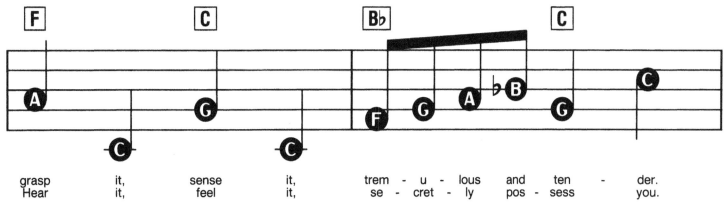

grasp   it,   sense   it,   trem - u - lous   and   ten - der.
Hear   it,   feel   it,   se - cret - ly   pos - sess   you.

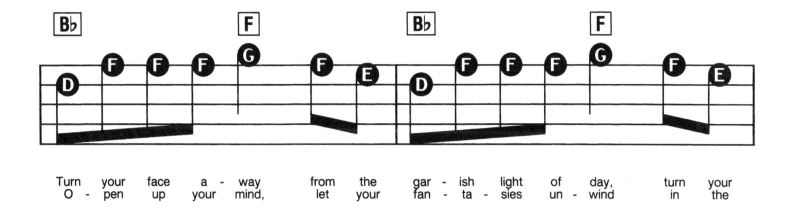

Turn   your   face   a - way   from   the   gar - ish   light   of   day,   turn   your
O - pen   up   your   mind,   let   your   fan - ta - sies   un - wind   in   the

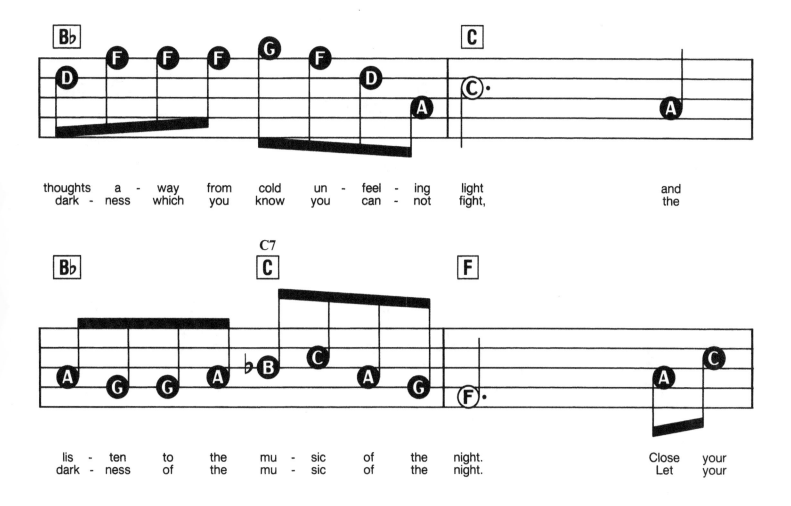

thoughts   a - way   from   cold   un - feel - ing   light   and
dark - ness   which   you   know   you   can - not   fight,   the

lis - ten   to   the   mu - sic   of   the   night.   Close   your
dark - ness   of   the   mu - sic   of   the   night.   Let   your

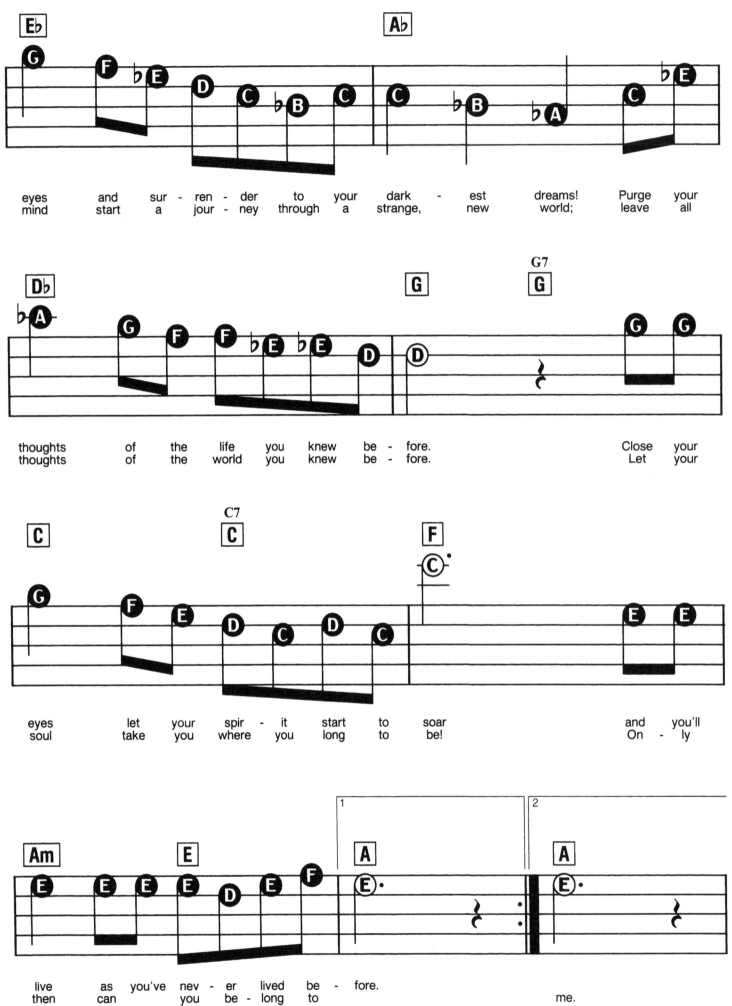

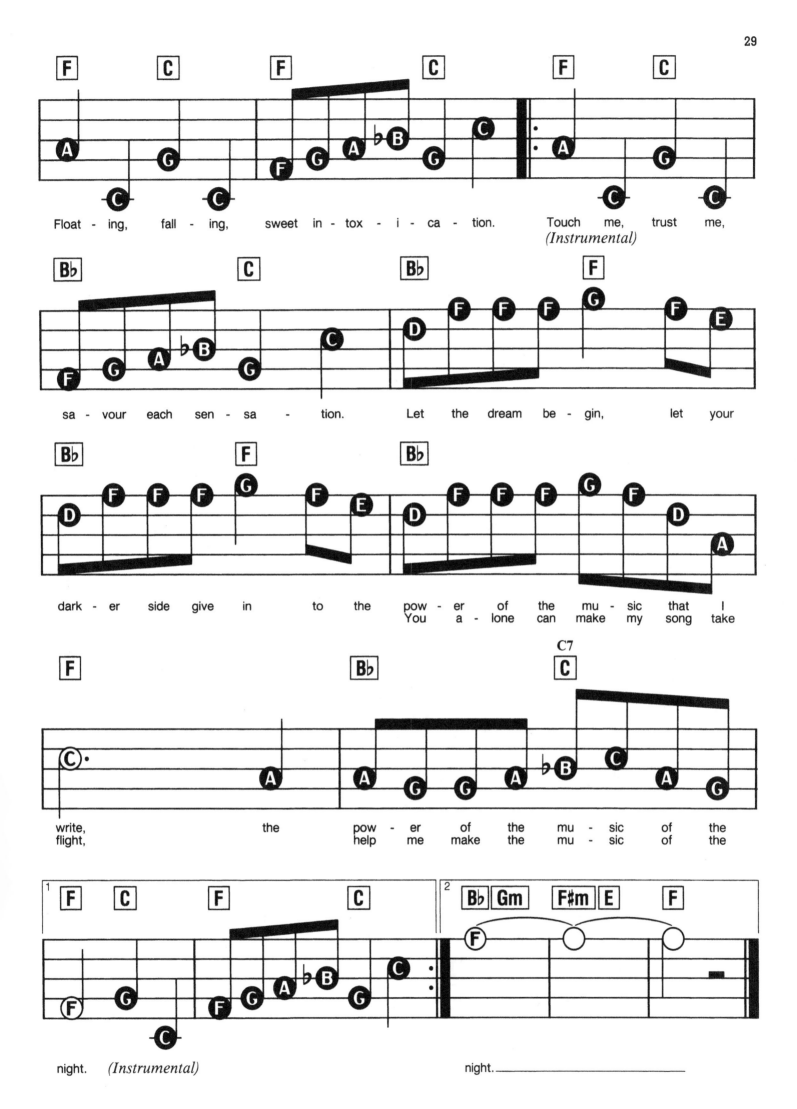

Prima Donna

Registration 3
Rhythm: Waltz

Music by Andrew Lloyd Webber
Lyrics by Charles Hart
Additional Lyrics by Richard Stilgoe

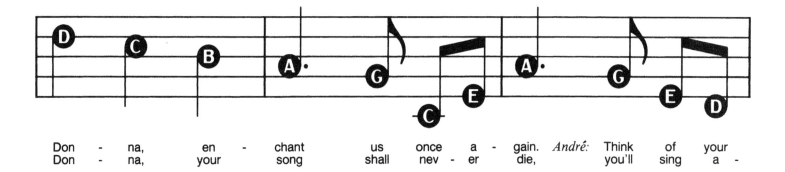

Don - na, en - chant us once a - gain. *André:* Think of your
Don - na, your song shall nev - er die, you'll sing a -

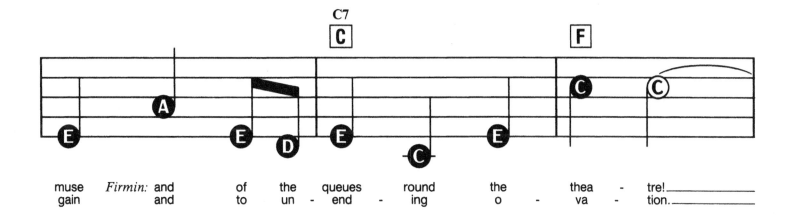

muse *Firmin:* and of the queues round the thea - tre!_____
gain and to un - end - ing o - va - tion._____

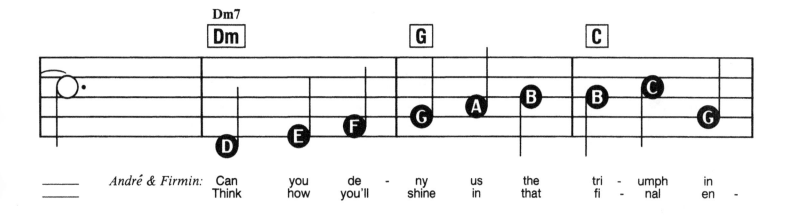

_____ *André & Firmin:* Can you de - ny us the tri - umph in
_____ Think how you'll shine in that fi - nal en -

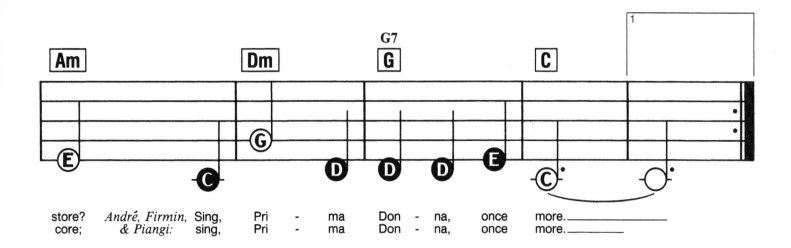

store? *André, Firmin,* Sing, Pri - ma Don - na, once more._____
core; *& Piangi:* sing, Pri - ma Don - na, once more._____

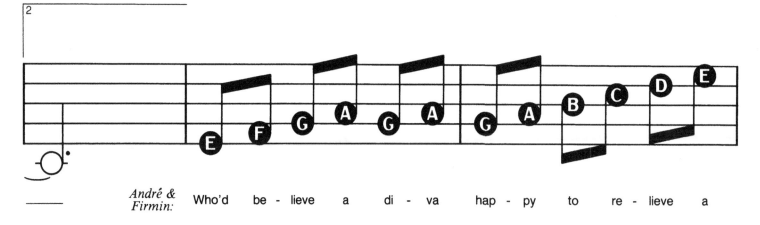

André & Firmin: Who'd be - lieve a di - va hap - py to re - lieve a

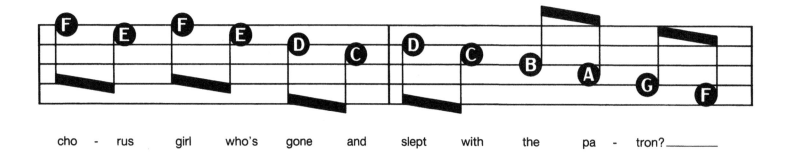

cho - rus girl who's gone and slept with the pa - tron?_____

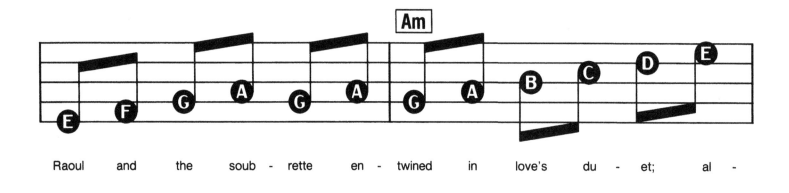

Raoul and the soub - rette en - twined in love's du - et; al -

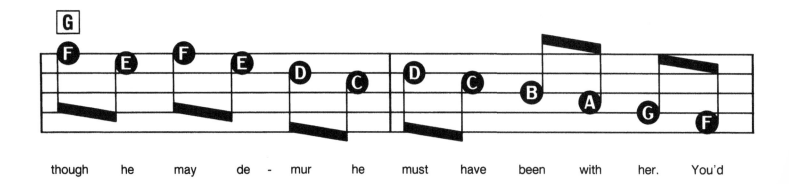

though he may de - mur he must have been with her. You'd

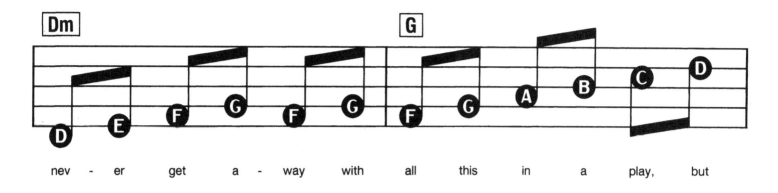

nev - er get a - way with all this in a play, but

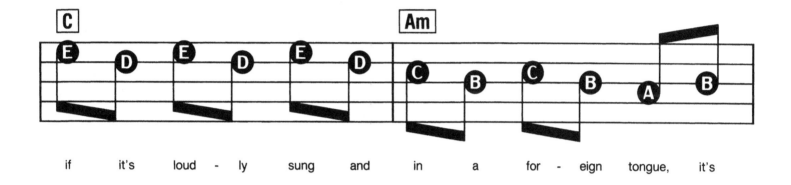

if it's loud - ly sung and in a for - eign tongue, it's

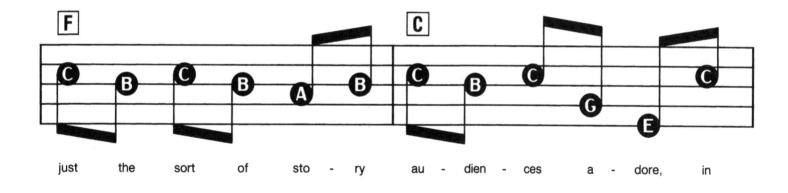

just the sort of sto - ry au - dien - ces a - dore, in

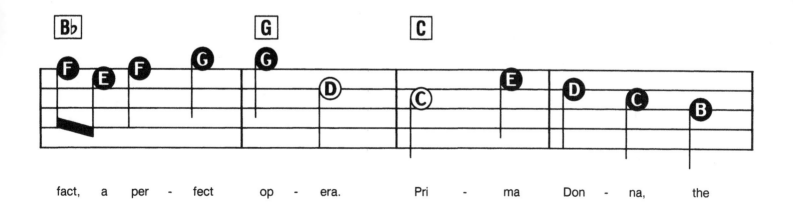

fact, a per - fect op - era. Pri - ma Don - na, the

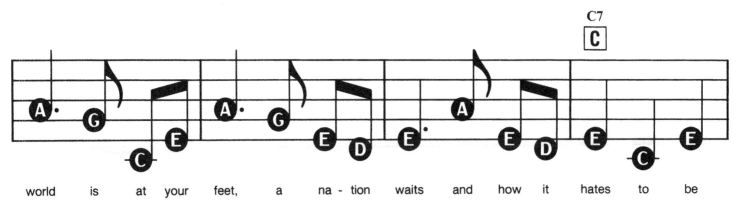

world is at your feet, a na - tion waits and how it hates to be

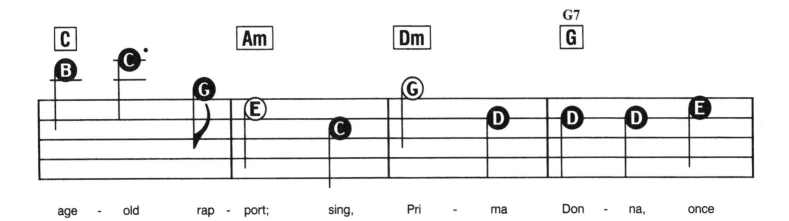

cheat - ed._____ *All:* Light up the stage with that

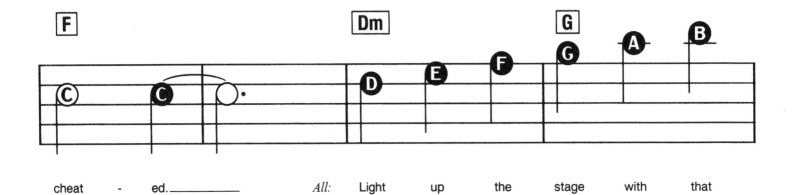

age - old rap - port; sing, Pri - ma Don - na, once

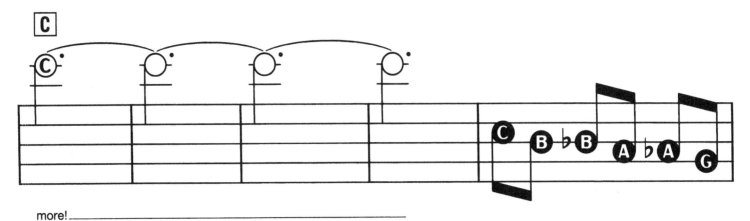

more!_____

Phantom (spoken): So... It is to be war between us!

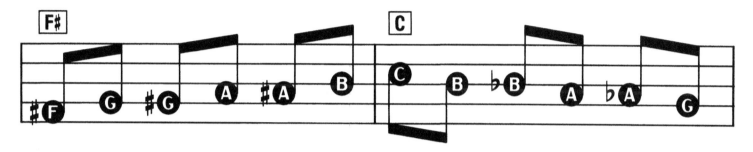

If these demands

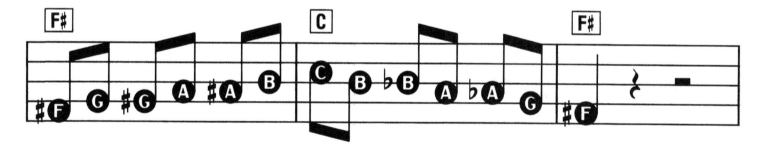

are not met   *a disaster beyond your imagination*

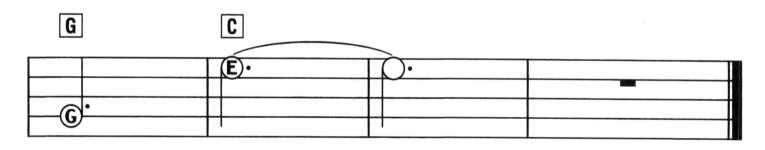

will occur.

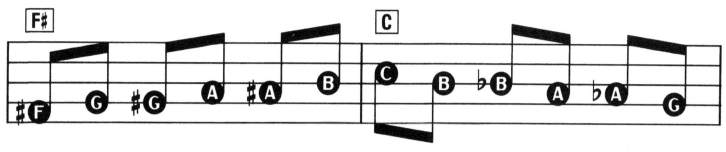

All: Once   more!_____

All I Ask of You

Registration 8
Rhythm: 8 Beat or Rock

Music by Andrew Lloyd Webber
Lyrics by Charles Hart
Additional Lyrics by Richard Stilgoe

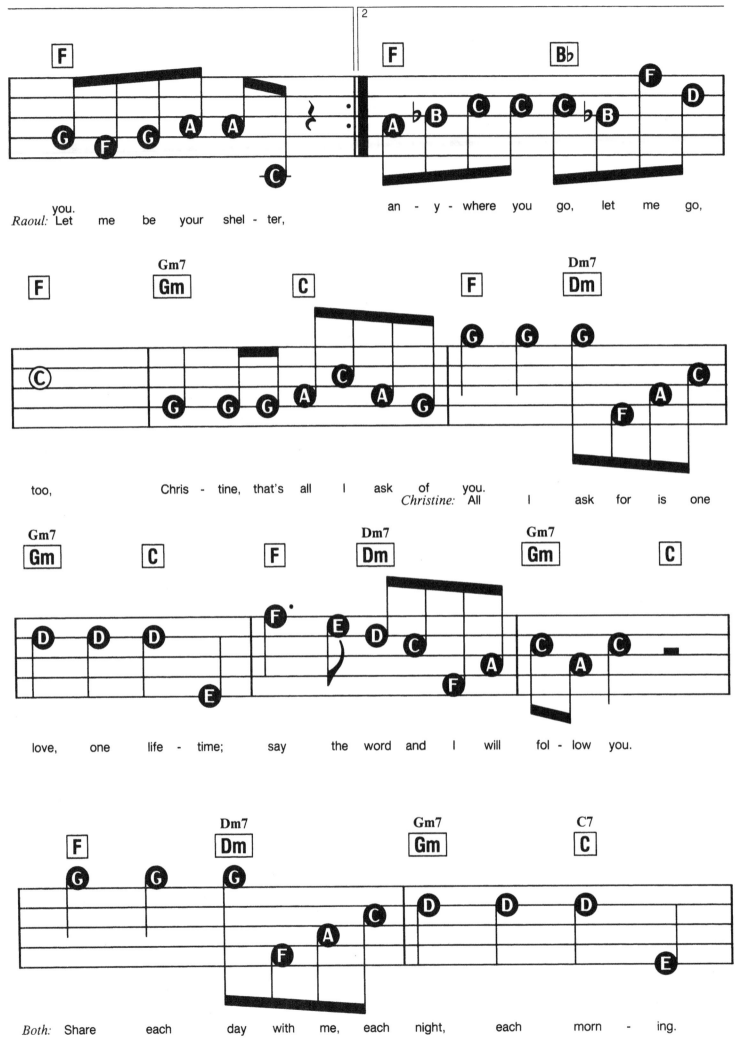

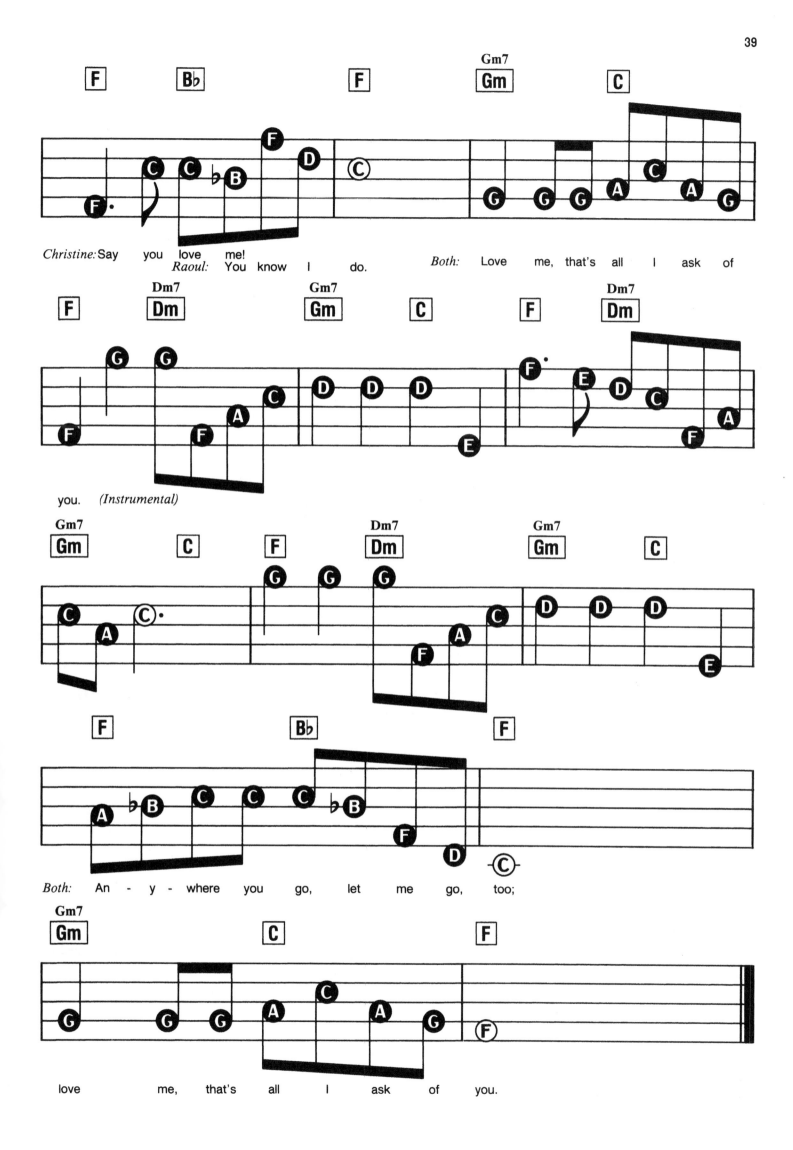

Christine: Say you love me! Raoul: You know I do. Both: Love me, that's all I ask of

you. (Instrumental)

Both: An - y - where you go, let me go, too;

love me, that's all I ask of you.

Masquerade

Registration 5
Rhythm: March or 8 Beat

Music by Andrew Lloyd Webber
Lyrics by Charles Hart
Additional Lyrics by Richard Stilgoe

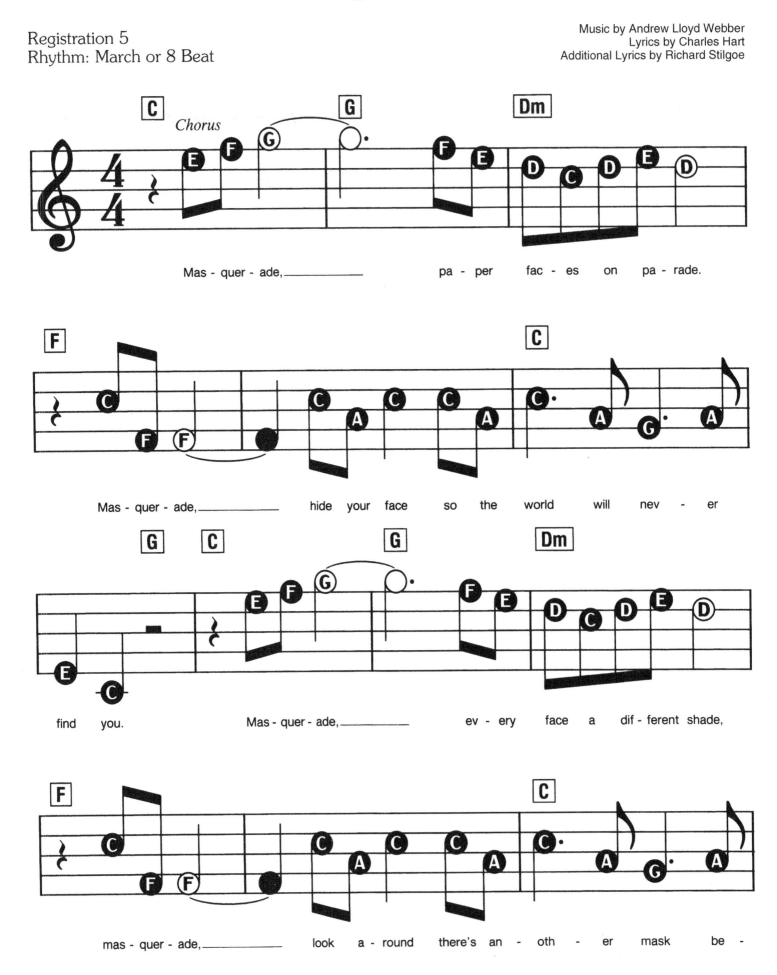

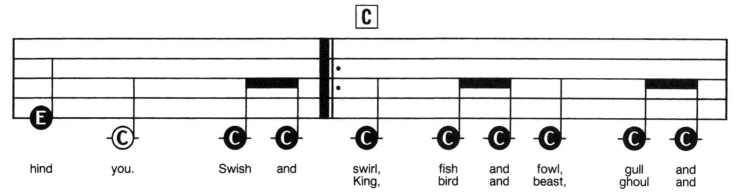

hind you. Swish and swirl, fish and fowl, gull and
King, bird and beast, ghoul and

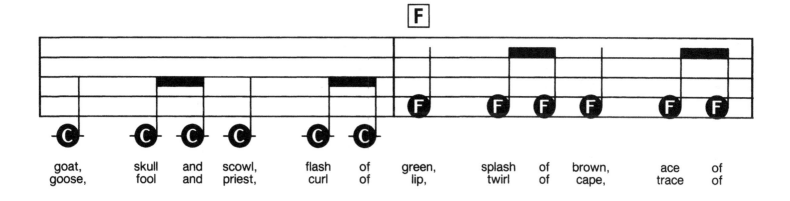

goat, skull and scowl, flash of green, splash of brown, ace of
goose, fool and priest, curl of lip, twirl of cape, trace of

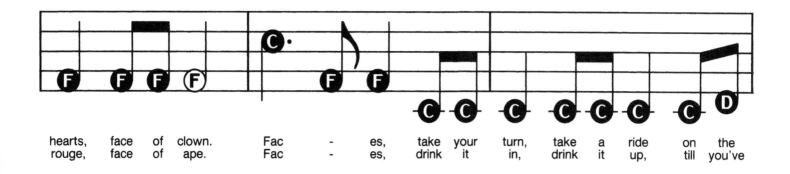

hearts, face of clown. Fac - es, take your turn, take a ride on the
rouge, face of ape. Fac - es, drink it in, drink it up, till you've

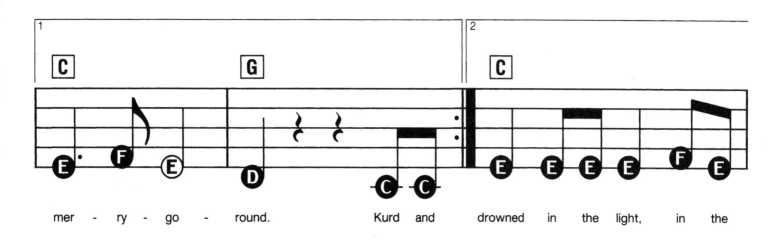

mer - ry - go - round. Kurd and drowned in the light, in the

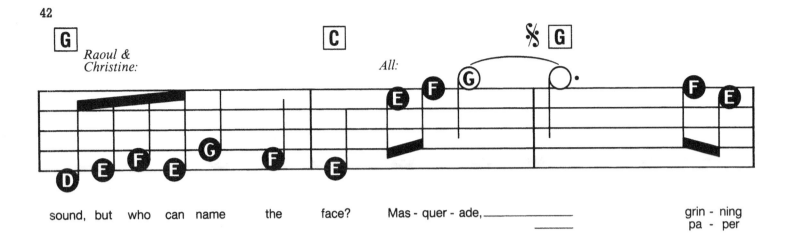

Raoul & Christine:
All:

sound, but who can name the face? Mas - quer - ade, _____ grin - ning
_____ pa - per

yel - low, spin - ning reds. Mas - quer - ade, _____ take your fill, let the
fac - es on pa - rade, mas - quer - ade, _____ hide your face, so the

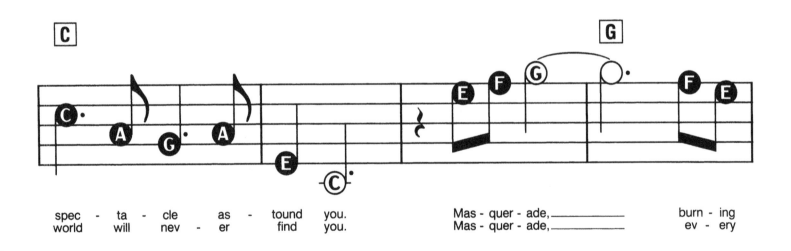

spec - ta - cle as - tound you. Mas - quer - ade, _____ burn - ing
world will nev - er find you. Mas - quer - ade, _____ ev - ery

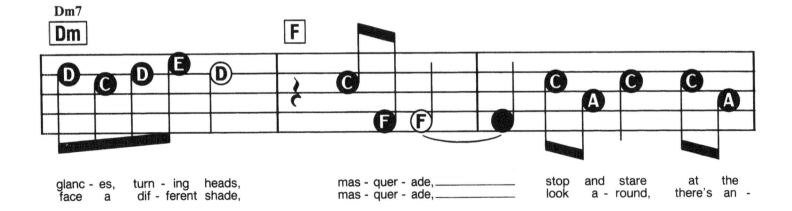

glanc - es, turn - ing heads, mas - quer - ade, _____ stop and stare at the
face a dif - ferent shade, mas - quer - ade, _____ look a - round, there's an -

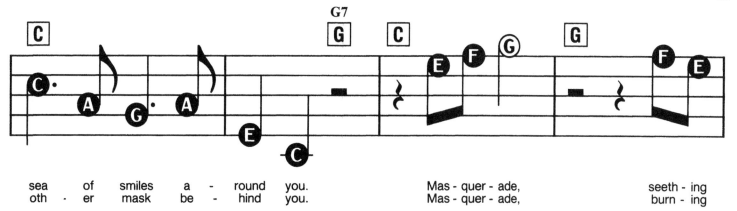

sea of smiles a - round you.
oth - er mask be - hind you.
Mas - quer - ade,
Mas - quer - ade,
seeth - ing
burn - ing

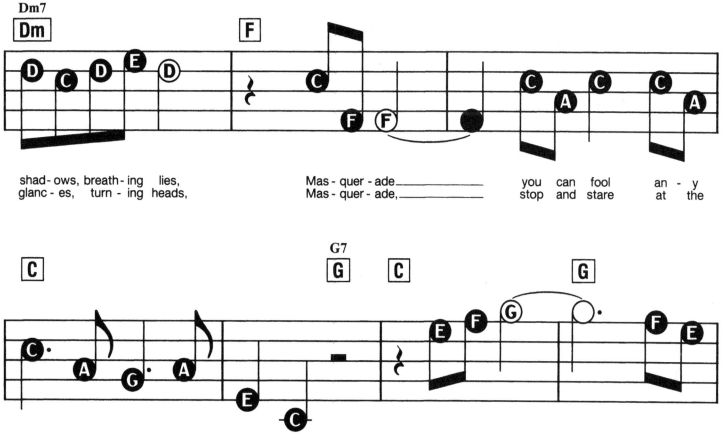

shad - ows, breath - ing lies,
glanc - es, turn - ing heads,
Mas - quer - ade_____
Mas - quer - ade,_____
you can fool an - y
stop and stare at the

friend who ev - er knew you.
sea of smiles a - round you.
Mas - quer - ade,_____
Mas - quer - ade,_____
leer - ing
grin - ning

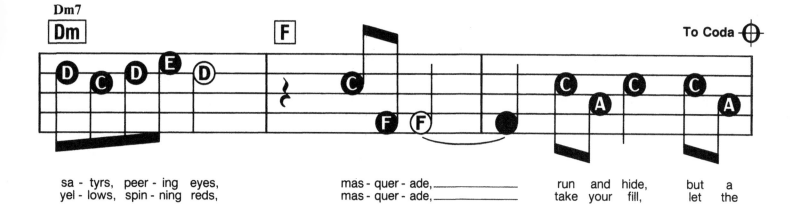

sa - tyrs, peer - ing eyes,
yel - lows, spin - ning reds,
mas - quer - ade,_____
mas - quer - ade,_____
run and hide, but a
take your fill, let the

44

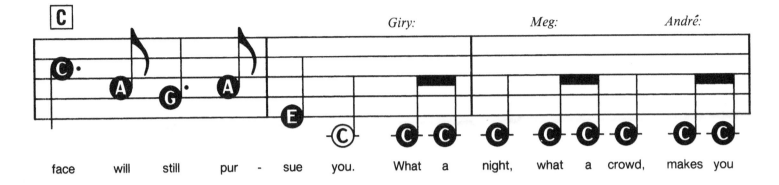

face will still pur - sue you. What a night, what a crowd, makes you

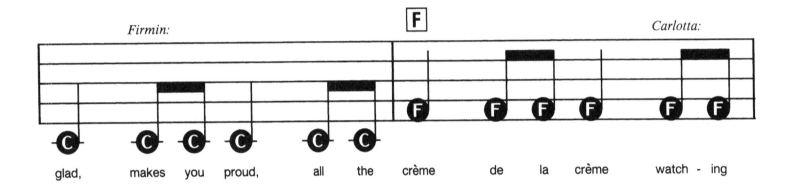

glad, makes you proud, all the crème de la crème watch - ing

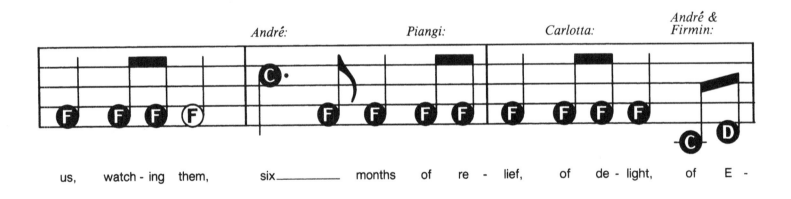

us, watch - ing them, six_____ months of re - lief, of de - light, of E -

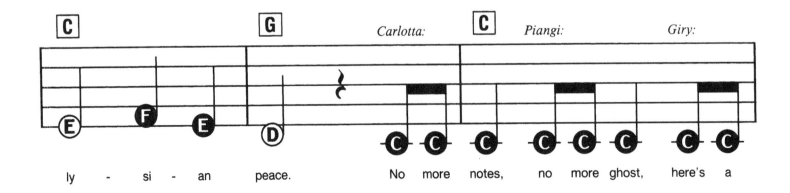

ly - si - an peace. No more notes, no more ghost, here's a

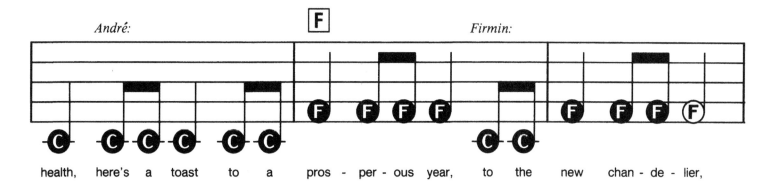

health, here's a toast to a pros - per - ous year, to the new chan - de - lier,

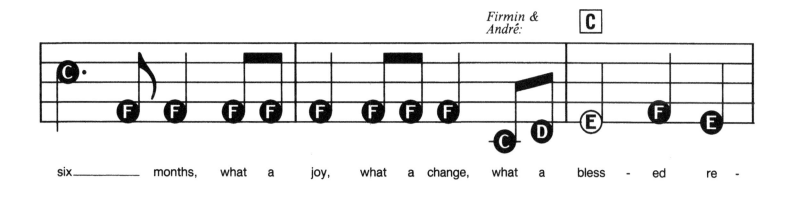

six_____ months, what a joy, what a change, what a bless - ed re -

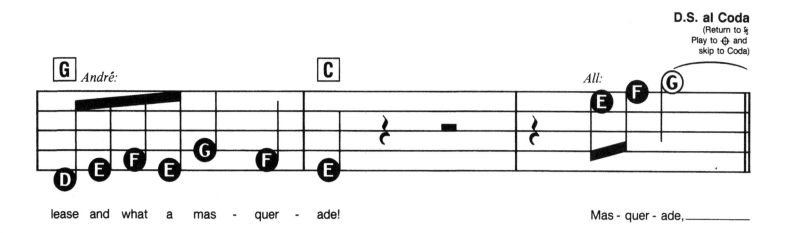

lease and what a mas - quer - ade!   Mas - quer - ade,_____

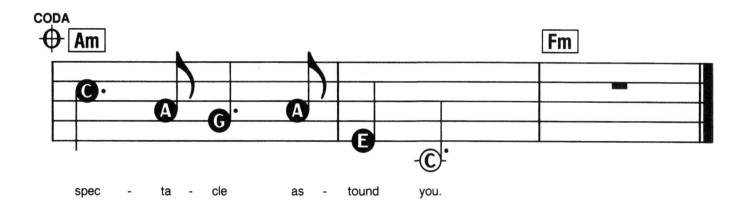

spec - ta - cle as - tound you.

The Fairground

Registration 7
Rhythm: None

Composed by
Andrew Lloyd Webber

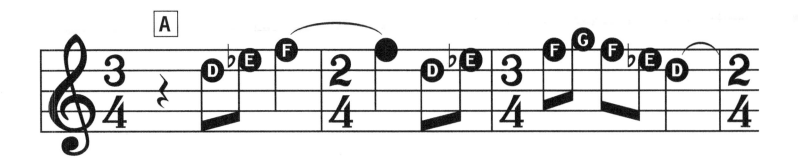

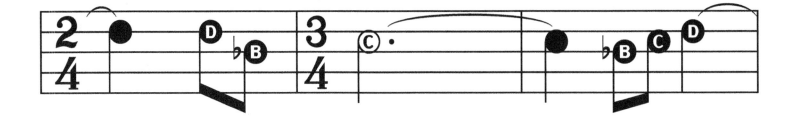

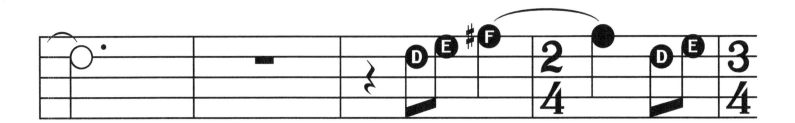

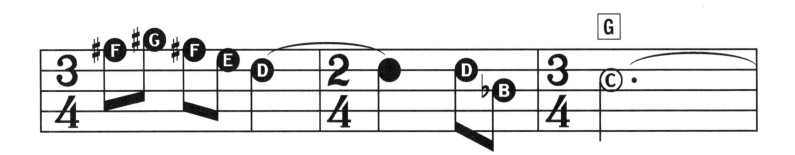

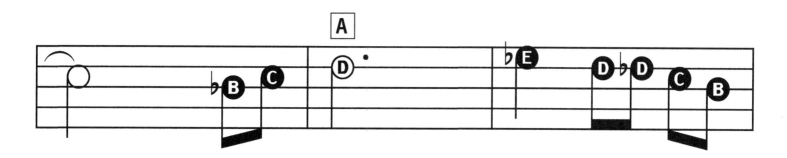

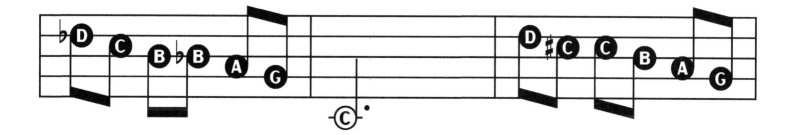

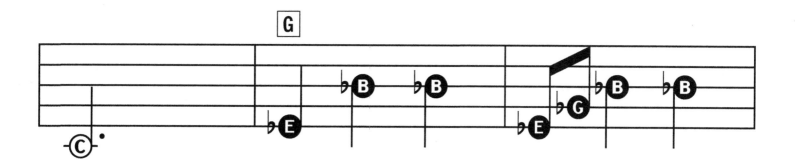

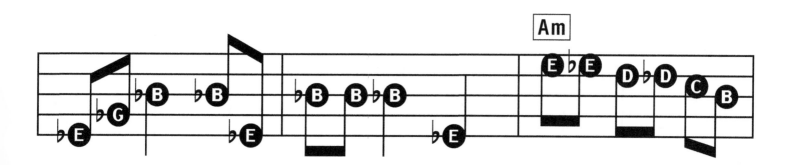

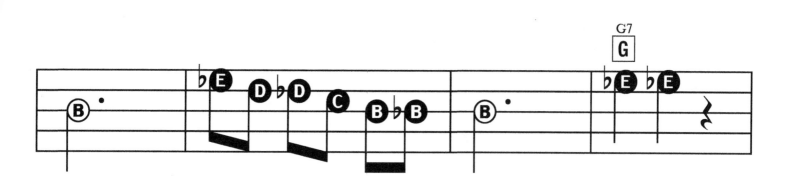

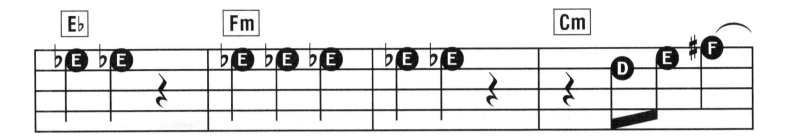

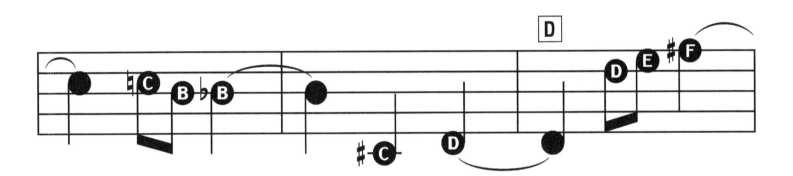

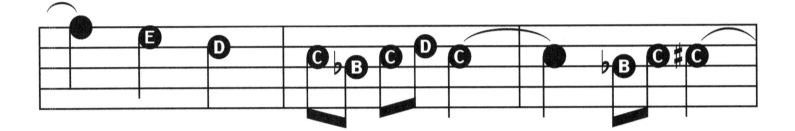

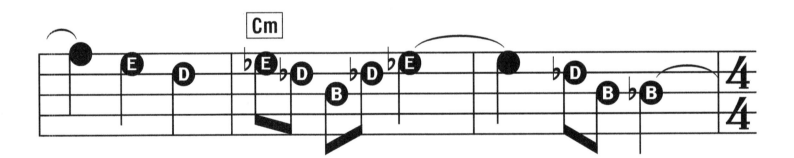

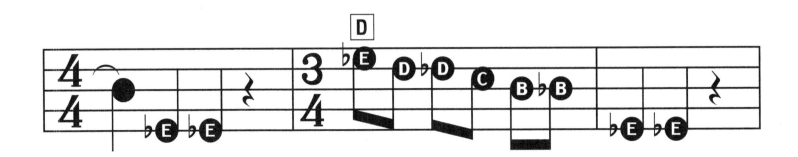

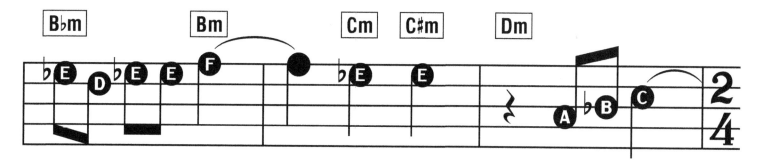

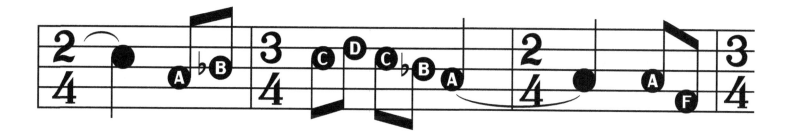

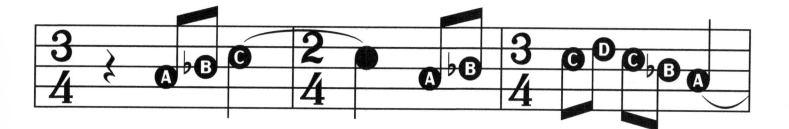

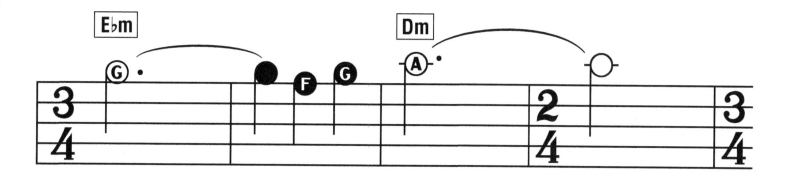

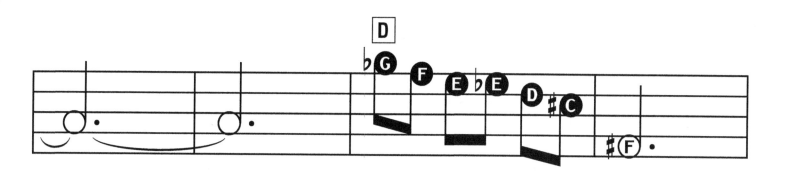

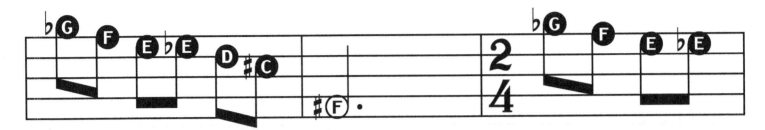

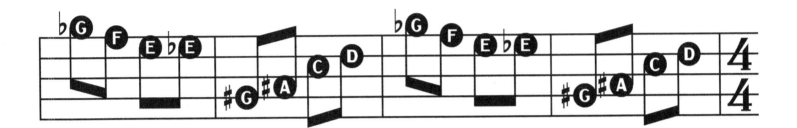

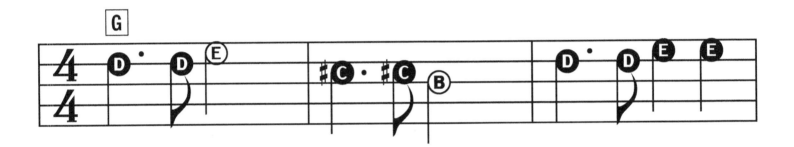

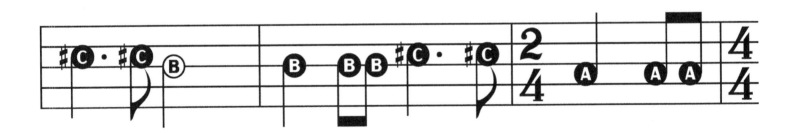

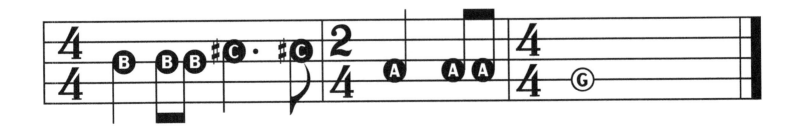

Journey to the Cemetery

Registration 8
Rhythm: 8 Beat or Rock

Composed by
Andrew Lloyd Webber

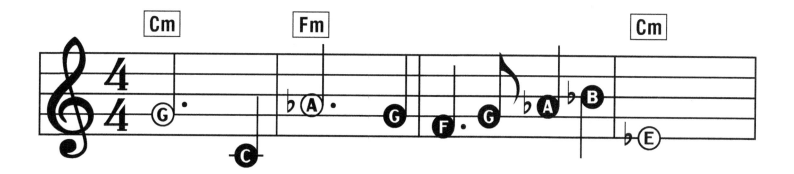

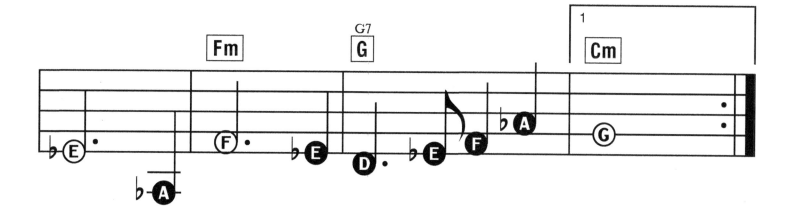

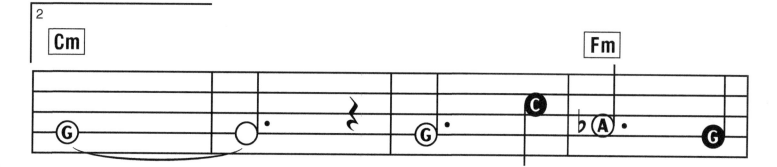

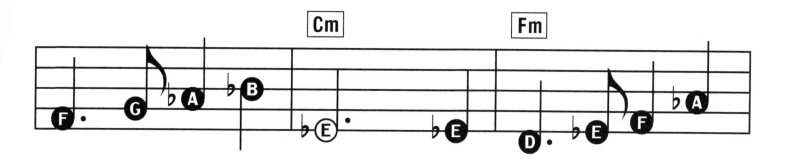

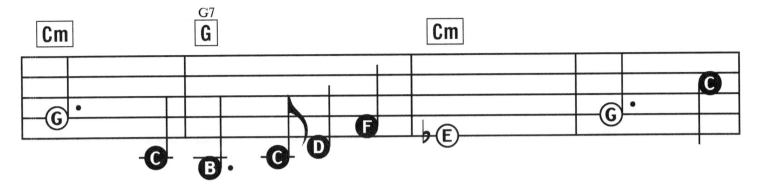

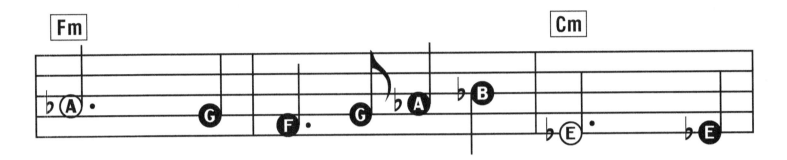

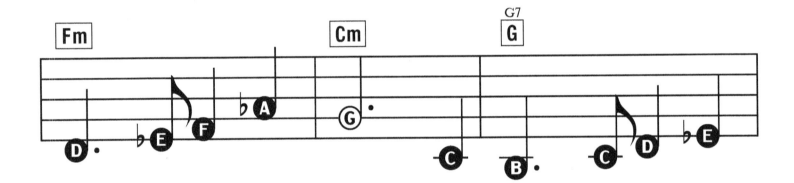

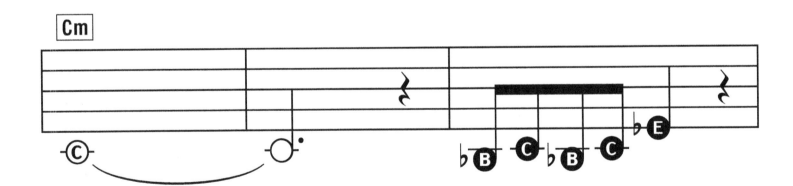

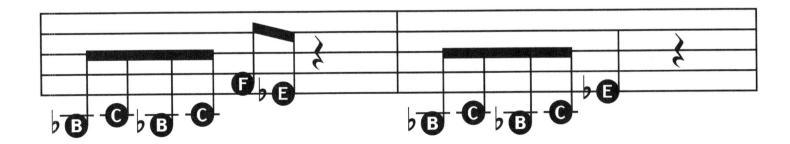

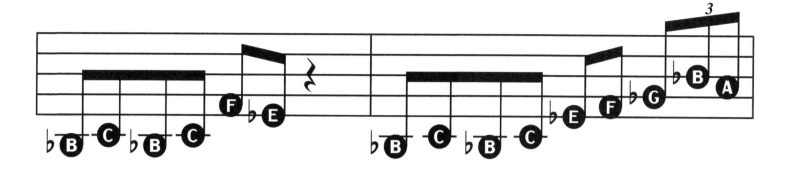

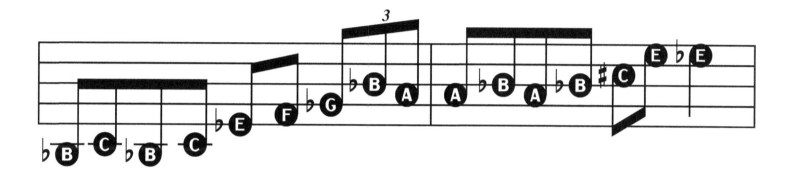

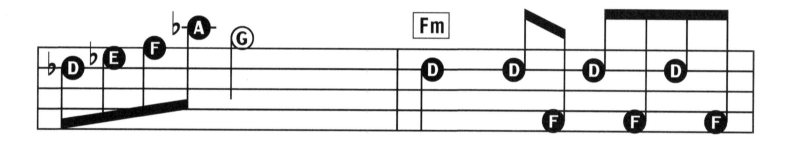

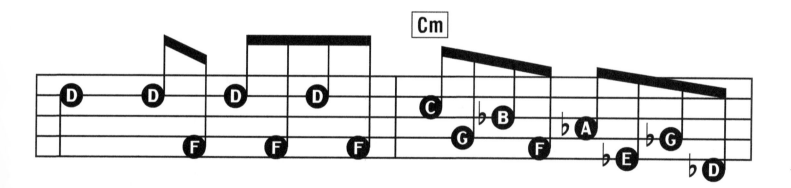

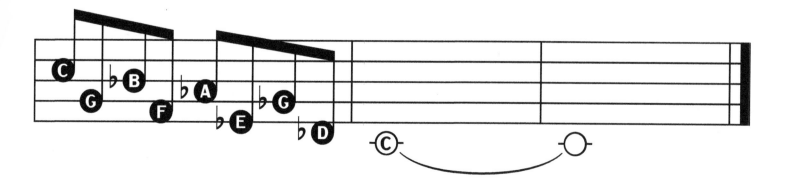

Wishing You Were Somehow Here Again

Registration 3
Rhythm: 8 Beat or Rock Ballad

Music by Andrew Lloyd Webber
Lyrics by Charles Hart
Additional Lyrics by Richard Stilgoe

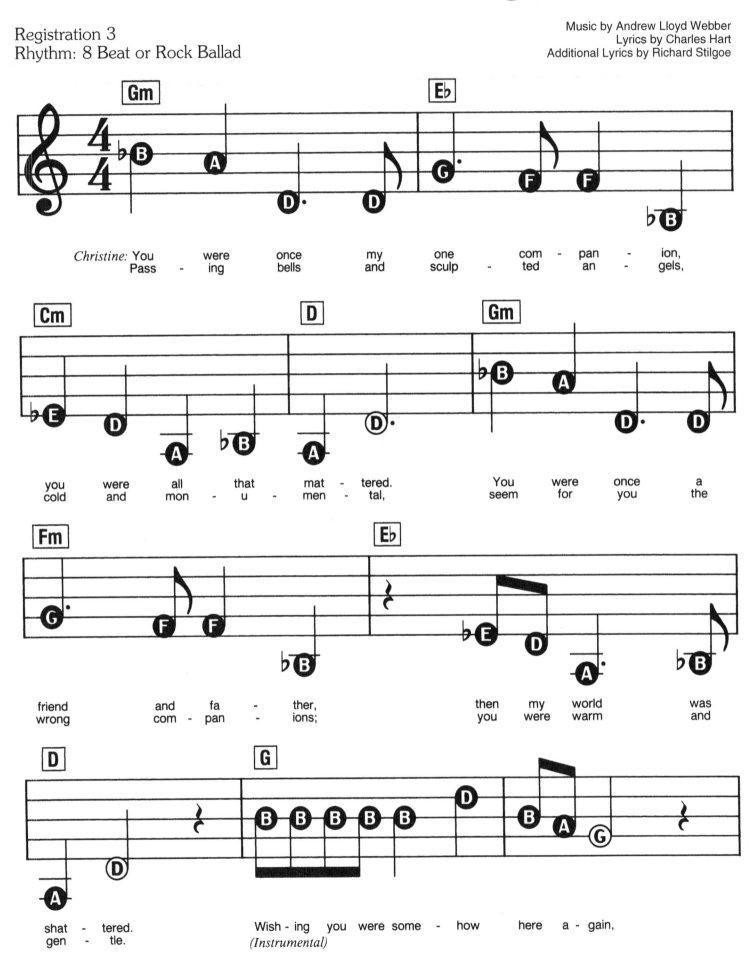

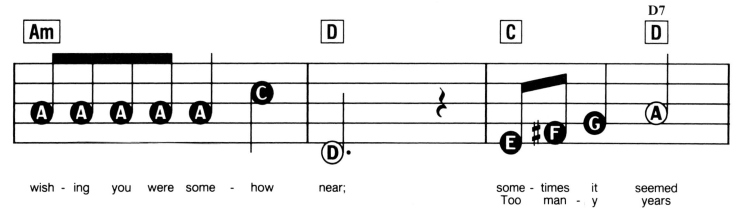

wish - ing you were some - how near;
Too man - y years

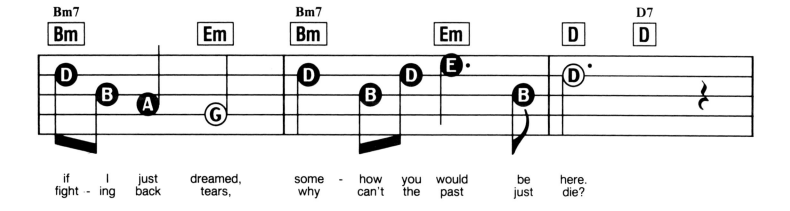

if I just dreamed, some - how you would be here.
fight - ing back tears, why can't the past just die?

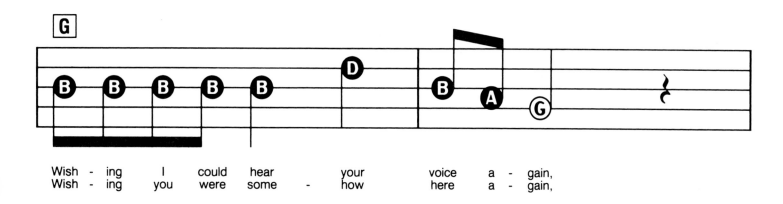

Wish - ing I could hear your voice a - gain,
Wish - ing you were some - how here a - gain,

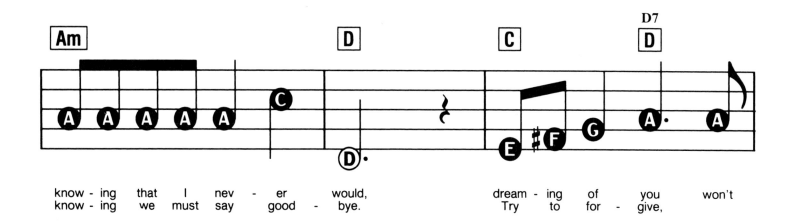

know - ing that I nev - er would, dream - ing of you won't
know - ing we must say good - bye. Try to for - give,

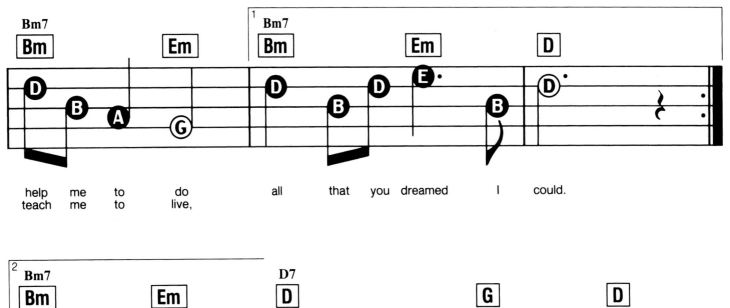

help me to do all that you dreamed I could.
teach me to live,

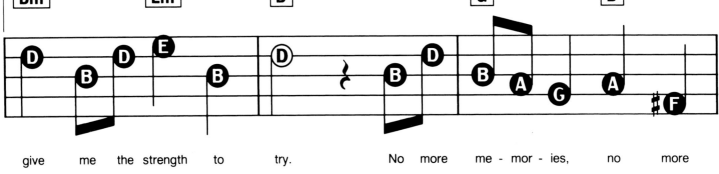

give me the strength to try. No more me - mor - ies, no more

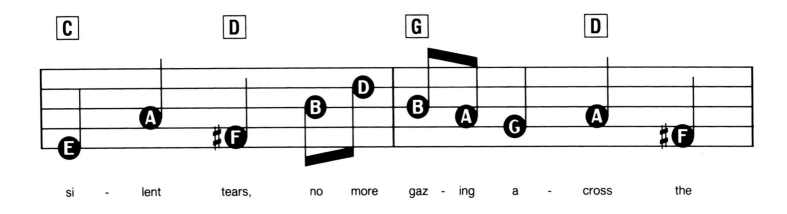

si - lent tears, no more gaz - ing a - cross the

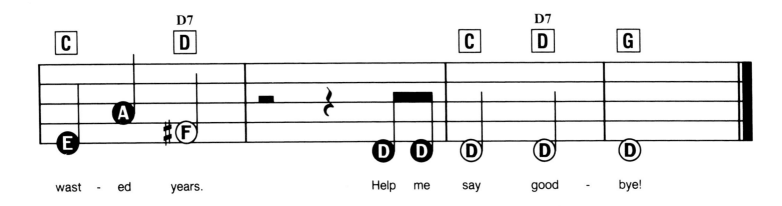

wast - ed years. Help me say good - bye!

The Point of No Return

Registration 1
Rhythm: Waltz

Music by Andrew Lloyd Webber
Lyrics by Charles Hart
Additional Lyrics by Richard Stilgoe

Phantom (as Don Juan):
Christine (as Aminta):

Gm	**A**	**Fm**
You	have	come
You	have	brought

Ebm	**Gm**	**A**	**Fm**	**Ebm**
here	in pur - suit of your deep - est	urge,
me	to that mo - ment where words run	dry,

Fm	**Dbm**	**Bm**
in pur - suit of that	wish which till	now has been
to that mo - ment where	speech dis - ap -	pears in - to

Am	**Gm**	**A**	**B**
si - lent,	si - lent.	I	have
si - lence,	si - lence.	I	have

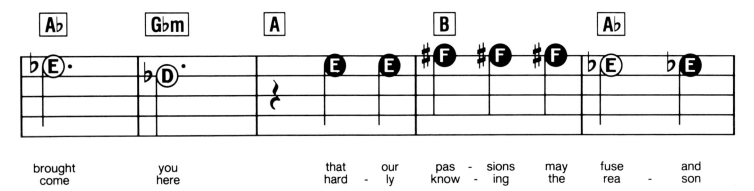

brought — you — that our pas - sions may fuse — and
come — here — hard - ly know - ing the rea - son

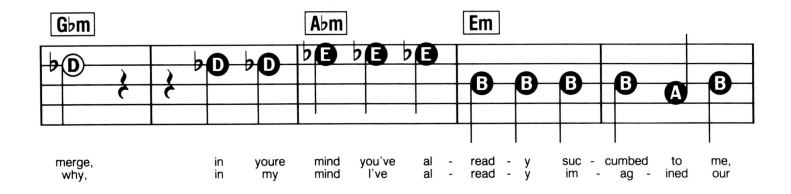

merge, — in youre mind you've al - read - y suc - cumbed to me,
why, — in my mind I've al - read - y im - ag - ined our

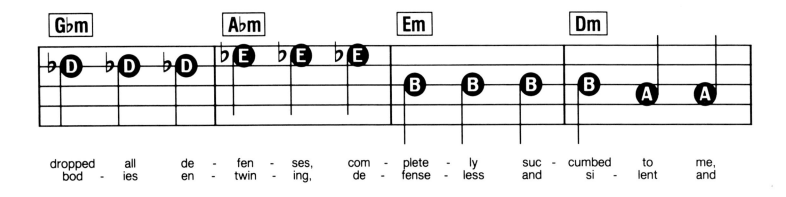

dropped all de - fen - ses, com - plete - ly suc - cumbed to me,
bod - ies en - twin - ing, de - fense - less and si - lent and

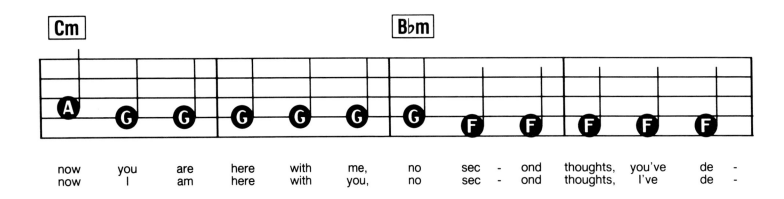

now you are here with me, no sec - ond thoughts, you've de -
now I am here with you, no sec - ond thoughts, I've de -

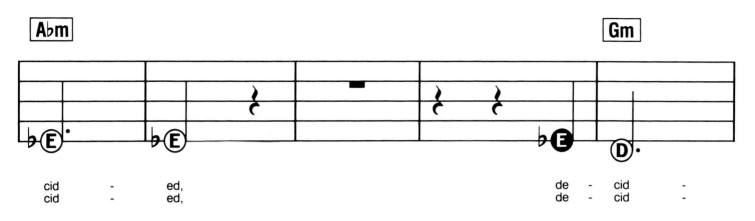

cid - ed,   de - cid -
cid - ed,   de - cid -

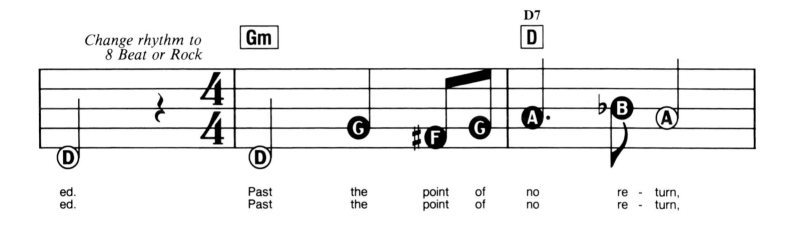

Change rhythm to 8 Beat or Rock

ed. Past the point of no re - turn,
ed. Past the point of no re - turn,

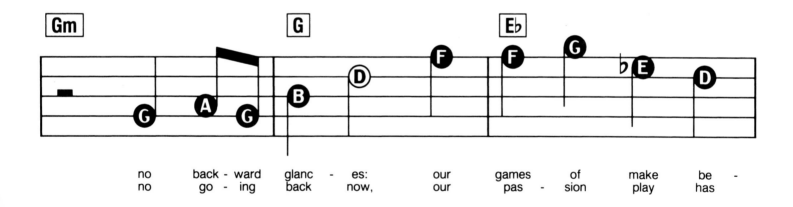

no back - ward glanc - es: our games of make be -
no go - ing back now, our pas - sion play has

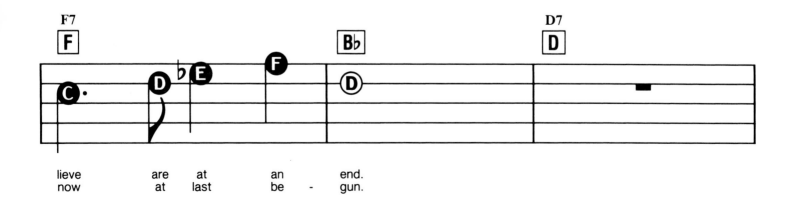

lieve are at an end.
now at last be - gun.

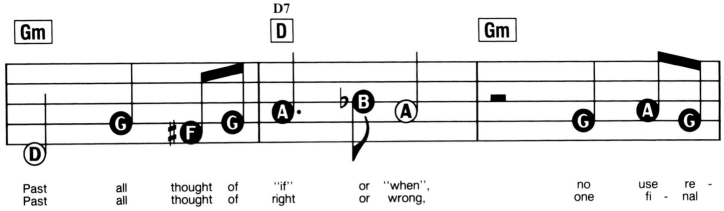

Past all thought of "if" or "when", no use re-
Past all thought of right or wrong, one fi - nal

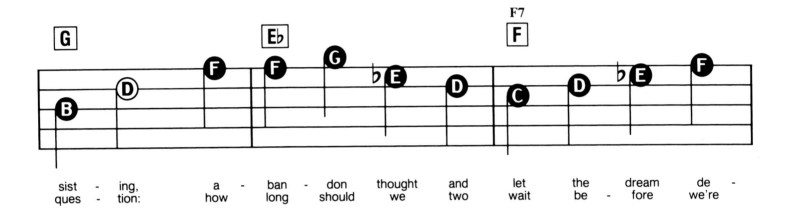

sist - ing, a - ban - don thought and let the dream de -
ques - tion: how long should we two wait be - fore we're

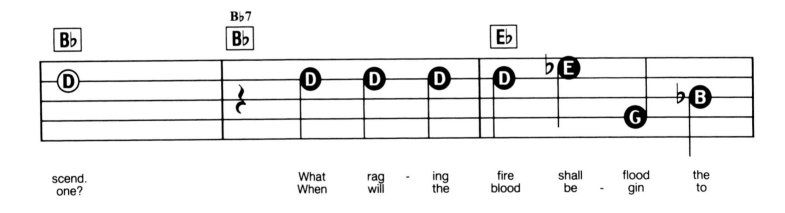

scend. What rag - ing fire shall flood the
one? When will the blood be - gin to

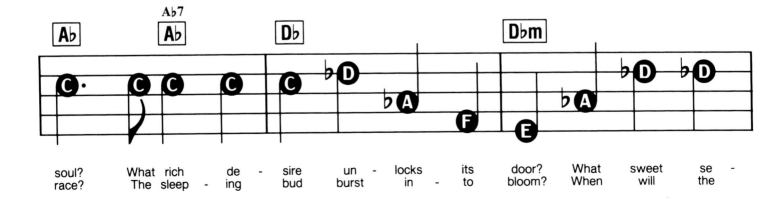

soul? What rich de - sire un - locks its door? What sweet se -
race? The sleep - ing bud burst in - to bloom? When will the

Learn to Be Lonely

Registration 3
Rhythm: 4/4 Ballad

Music by Andrew Lloyd Webber
Lyrics by Charles Hart

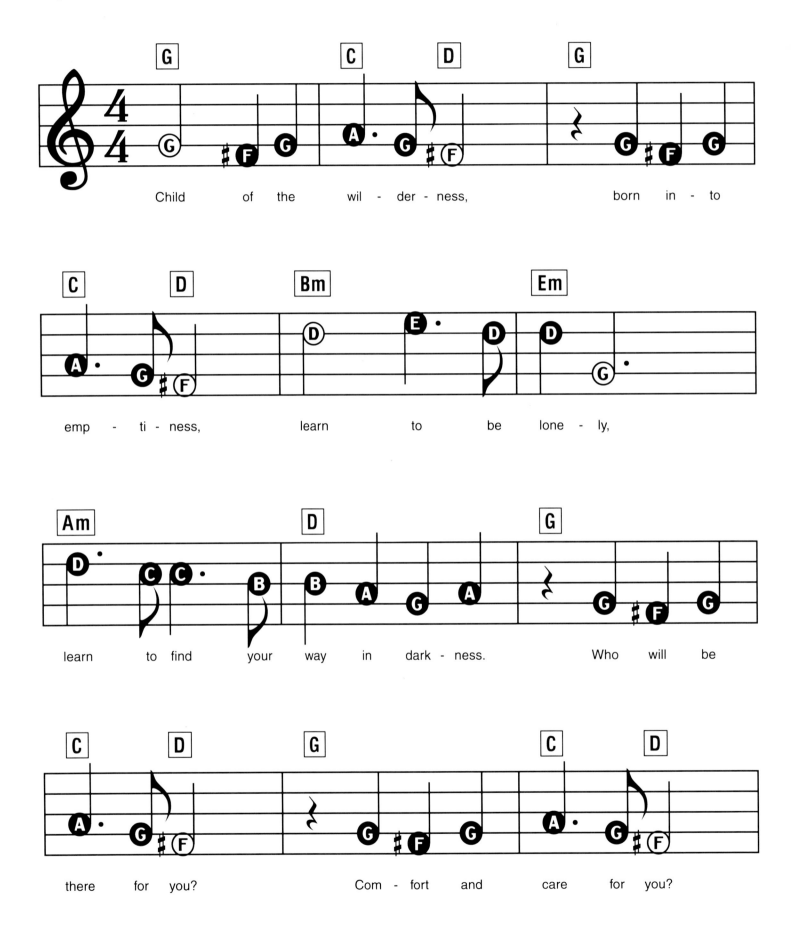

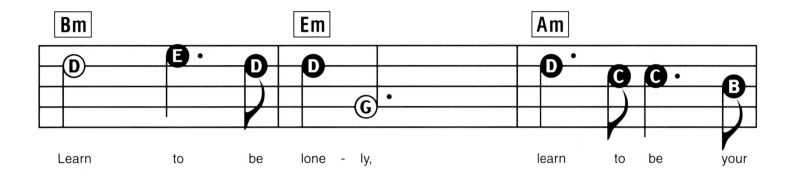

Learn to be lone - ly, learn to be your

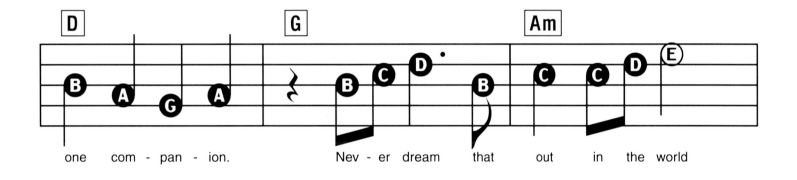

one com - pan - ion. Nev - er dream that out in the world

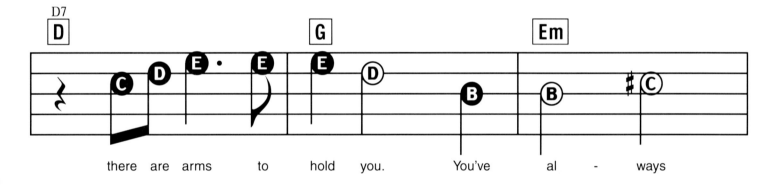

there are arms to hold you. You've al - ways

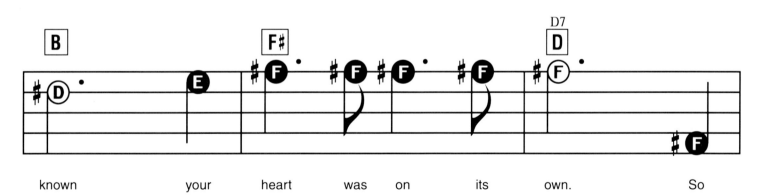

known your heart was on its own. So

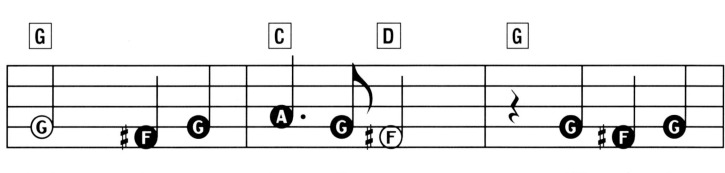

laugh in your lone - li - ness, child of the

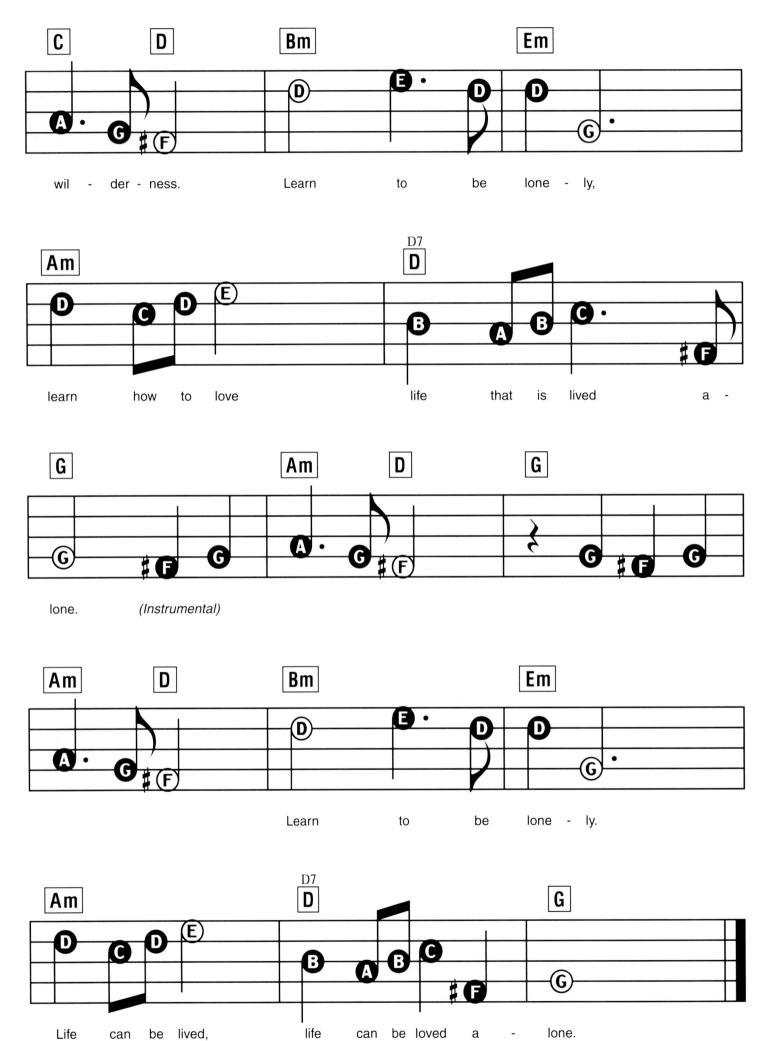